THE
TIME
TRAP

THE
TIME
TRAP

Third Edition

Alec Mackenzie

AMACOM
American Management Association

New York • Atlanta • Boston • Chicago • Kansas City • San Francisco • Washington, D.C.
Brussels • Mexico City • Tokyo • Toronto

Library of Congress Cataloging-in-Publication Data

Mackenzie, R. Alec.
    The time trap / Alec Mackenzie. — 3rd ed.
        p.   cm.
    Includes bibliographical references and index.
    ISBN 0-8144-7926-X (pbk.)
    1. Time management.   I. Title.
HD69.T54M33   1997
650.1—dc21   97-20780
                                              CIP

The material on pages 168–169 is adapted from Ralph G. Nichols and Leonard A.
Stevens, Are You Listening? McGraw-Hill Book Company, © 1957, and is
reproduced by permission.

Printing number

20 19 18 17 16 15

Contents

Preface to the Third Edition

I have been studying how we use our time for more than twenty years. In those years, I have led workshops and seminars about time management in forty countries to approximately 50,000 people in almost every major industry and profession. I have met with managers of hundreds of companies around the world, to help them improve how time is used within their organizations. In the process of writing six books and more than sixty journal articles about time management, I have interviewed scores of businesspeople about the time problems they encounter.

The remarkable thing I have learned from discussing time management with so many different people is how similar the problems are. By and large, we all tend to have the same kinds of difficulties with time. An attorney is just as apt to take on too much—and then have trouble accomplishing all her commitments—as a school principal is. A sales manager can easily have an entire day fractured with phone calls—and so can a beauty shop manager. The owner of a print shop in Perth Amboy is just as reluctant to turn an important project over to someone else as the director of a research lab in Amsterdam is. The finance manager of a multinational entertainment company is swamped with work because the department is understaffed—just like the owner of a small retail shop whose one employee just quit.

All these people are hampered by quite similar "time wasters," my name for anything that prevents you from achieving your objectives most effectively. I can recite the time wasters of people from diverse backgrounds and different countries in different types of enterprises and at varying levels of responsibility—and they will, with very few exceptions, be almost indistinguishable. Take a look at this list:

1. Attempting too much at once
2. Procrastinating
3. Doing it myself (that is, not delegating)
4. Not saying no
5. Personal disorganization (cluttered desk)

Can you tell who might have assembled this list of time concerns? Could it be the head bookkeeper? The junior art director? The vice-president of marketing? The management trainee at the bank? The owner of the auto parts store? The unit secretary in the hospital ward? Could it, perhaps, be you? In fact, this list is taken from a compilation of the ten "winners" listed by a group of forty presidents of electrical contracting firms. These CEOs have the same difficulties with time that anyone else does.

The truth is that we are all alike, at least in our handling of time. I consider this good news. It means that we can learn from each other. And that, to a very large degree, is what this book is: a sharing of knowledge and ideas collected from businesspeople all over the world.

One of the foundations of this book is what I call the international profile of time wasters. It represents accumulated data on time concerns from thousands of businesspeople worldwide, and it came about this way. As we worked with companies to help them improve their overall time usage, we were always asked, "But where do we start? What do we work on first?" The obvious answer was: "Whatever are your biggest problems." So we set out to learn what they were.

As a first step, all those involved in a company's workshop name their own personal ten biggest time problems, taken from a list of forty possibilities. Then they assign a weighting: Their most serious individual problem gets a 10, the next most serious gets a 9, and so on. Then we take all the rankings and combine them, to get a "profile" of the entire organization. Then we concentrate on making improvements in those that rank the highest. We do essentially the same thing in seminars, asking participants to rank their personal time concerns.

Over the years, we have combined all the company profiles, and all the individual rankings from seminars, and so have developed a global composite of the most common time problems. There are some minor differences among various countries, but generally speaking the same kinds of problems haunt everyone, and pretty much to the same degree.

Part Two of *The Time Trap* presents the top twenty time wasters. It is much more than a laundry list of problems: It also presents practical, realistic, field-tested solutions. The good news is that, just as people share the same problems, the same kinds of solutions work for those problems. So you can benefit from the experience of all those others who have wrestled with your time concerns.

This may tempt you to turn to Part Two right away, and start working on your biggest problem areas, one at a time. But please resist. The problem of time management is complex, with multiple interconnections and overlapping results; our habits in one area can affect our behaviors in another. Piecemeal changes produce piecemeal results—at best.

I urge you to start the book at the beginning: Part One. Here you will learn the underlying principles that make everything else work. Part One describes the big picture, the how and the why; Part Two goes into the details, the what. If you try to do things the other way around, you will be far less effective. It would be like starting to build your vacation cabin by crafting the bathroom window because you had learned about stained glass—with no house design, no blueprints, no foundation, no budget, no schedule. You'd probably end up with a nice window, but would it ever fit into the house?

In Part One we try to understand why time management is still a problem, after all these years. We look at the very powerful pull of human nature, and the difficulty of learning new habits. We also expand our thinking about time management: It's not about time per se, but about the benefits we derive in our life from better usage of time, especially in four "breakthrough" areas: productivity, stress prevention, balance between work and personal life, and progress toward our goals. Throughout the book, we have also integrated material addressing time management concerns that face the self-employed, who now, according to some studies constitute thirty percent of the workforce.

We then get into the fundamentals of taking charge of your time. We learn that managing time starts with establishing goals, and that the ability to set priorities is essential in the real world, where things have a way of changing. I will show you the single most effective time management tool: a written plan for the day, and the overall planning system that it supports.

Part One, in other words, presents all the general concepts you should have under your belt before starting on the specifics in Part Two.

Then in Part Two you meet the twenty top time wasters. For each one, we define the real problem, examine the root causes, and then delve into solution strategies. In many cases you will "witness" a typical scene in which the particular time concern is causing a problem—or is about to.

To a large degree, many of us find ourselves in trouble with time because we simply do not know what to say in difficult situations. So we end up saying yes when we didn't want to, we allow other people to interrupt us because we don't want to offend them, we accept confusing instructions from the boss because we don't want to appear stupid . . . and we end up falling further and further behind. In Part Two you will find help. Here are dozens of mini-scenarios, taken from the real world but fictionalized, showing you exactly what to say to improve the situation; some are for bosses, some for team members.

Each Time Topic in Part Two concludes with a "mini-audit" called Check Yourself, by which you can rate yourself on how well you do with each time waster. Ask yourself the questions and make a record of your ratings. This will tell you how you're doing overall with each time concern, and will also indicate specific aspects that you need to concentrate on. Then, after working on your action plan for a while, try the audit again and see how much you improve.

Also in Part Two you will find visual note cards emphasizing particular techniques. They are intended to serve as both highlighters and quick recovery tools, enabling you to go back and retrieve a key idea.

In Part Three, you meet contemporary top time managers

as they apply the principles of time management in their own lives. Then Part Three leads you through the process of developing your personal action plan for getting rid of time wasters in your life, after you have studied each time waster and tested yourself in Part Two.

Appendix A contains an at-a-glance summary of the twenty top time concerns. A complete list of causes and solutions is given for each one, including additional hints that do not appear in the main chapter. Appendix B talks about the various options and considerations in using electronic time management systems.

If you believe that time is mastering you instead of you mastering it, if you've made tentative efforts in the past to control time but are not satisfied with the results, and if you wish to claim the biggest benefits that time has to offer, then read on. My best wishes for making your time usage more productive and more rewarding.

A.M.

Acknowledgments

I wish to thank Shirley Long, a gifted prose and screenplay writer from Ankeny, Iowa, who has contributed substantially to many of my time management projects over the years. She was highly instrumental in bringing this book to fruition.

I would also like to thank Barbara Ashley, my personal assistant, whose diplomatic and organizational skills are unsurpassed. Her contributions were significant throughout the time we worked on this book

Thanks also to Billie Sorensen, whose help was invaluable as we developed the original classic principles of time management. Thanks also to Jacquie Flynn, Development Editor at AMACOM Books, and to Mary Glenn for their consultation on content, and to Richard Gatjens for his gracious and effective editing.

Part One

Time Management in the Year 2000 and Beyond

One

Why Is Time Management Still a Problem?

"I just didn't have enough time."

Yes you did. You had all the time there is. You had the same twenty-four hours, the same 1,440 minutes, that everyone else did. But you didn't have the skills of managing the time that was available to you.

Have you ever said to yourself, There just aren't enough hours in the day?

Do you agree with this statement: If you want things done right, you have to do them yourself.

Do you often feel frustrated because you are unable to finish important jobs? Do you ever look at the clock and realize with a slight sense of panic that it's almost 5 P.M. and you haven't really gotten started on what you wanted to accomplish today?

When critical tasks are needed, such as year-end reports, do you find yourself working long nights and weekends to complete them? And do you sometimes miss the deadline anyway?

Have you ever decided to take on another important project, even though you are already feeling overloaded, because it's too important to assign to anyone else?

Do you have a vague sense that something is wrong with the way you do things but you can't say exactly what it is?

If you identify with most of these statements, you do indeed have a problem with time. If it's any comfort, you are not alone. Most people have difficulties with time management.

But why? After all, "time management" is not a new idea. Since the original version of *The Time Trap* was published in 1972, there has been a landslide of information about time. There are dozens of books and hundreds of magazine articles on the subject. Articles with "new" ideas on how to use time better show up in magazines from *Business Week* to *Progressive Farmer*, and practically everything in between. We have scholarly studies of managerial motivation in psychology journals, discussions of productivity and effectiveness in business journals, and how-to advice in publications geared toward specific professions, and time-saving tips proliferate in general-interest magazines.

But that's just the beginning. There are practically unlimited opportunities for seminars and workshops on how to get control of your time. My guess is that if you hold any kind of management position in a medium-size or larger company, you receive promotional information on time management seminars at least once a week. And if you can't take the time away to attend a seminar, never fear: There are literally hundreds of packaged programs that you can use on your own—videotapes, films, audiotapes you can listen to in the car, and self-managed learning modules of all kinds.

There's more. Almost an entire industry has been built up to serve the person who "just can't seem to get organized." Stop in any stationery store, and you'll find a wide assortment of desk calendars, pocket diaries, "things-to-do-today" notepads—and of course the many full-blown "organizer" systems, with imitation leather covers, pockets for pencils and small calculators, and brightly colored separator tabs so you can add information in any category under the sun.

And many of us take this approach one giant step further and use time management software on our personal computers to keep track of all the details we used to put in our appointment calendar, to-do lists, and personal organizers. With these software systems, we make automatic updates in our calendar, coordinate meetings with associates, monitor project deadlines, and keep track of our personal time usage—all with lightning speed.

And yet, after all these years, and with all these innovations, we are still caught in the time trap. With this mountain of information, these dazzling new tools, we still groan and say, "There just isn't enough time!" Why is this? Why is it that we still find ourselves making some of the classic time management mistakes, even though we know better? The answer is simple—and very complex: human nature.

The Powerful Pull of Human Nature

The fundamental causes of much of our problems with time can be traced to some powerful tendencies of human nature. Practically all the "rules" of time management are contradictory to the laws of human nature. And those strong psychological tugs make it difficult to do what we know we should do. Let's look at some of the ways human nature traps us.

Martin knows all about delegation. It is, after all, one of the basic tenets of management. So when he is presented with responsibility for a new project, he knows he should assign it to the systems analyst in the department; she is fully capable, and has room in her work schedule. But Martin is reluctant. He used to be a systems analyst himself, and he knows exactly how this job should be done. He may not fully appreciate that what he is feeling is a subconscious need for psychological comfort. It would be more rewarding to do this task—which he is thoroughly comfortable with—than to supervise someone else, which he hasn't much experience with. He may be a bit jealous of the other analyst's talents. Also, because he is new in his current position, he wants to make a strong impression as a top achiever; what better way than with this important new project?

Sarah is a copywriter in an advertising agency—and so she is used to living with deadlines. She knows how to concentrate on the task at hand and get work done under the gun. She has just one problem: folks who drop in to visit. Mostly it's other people in the creative department at the agency; often it's the art director she's usually teamed up with. On some level she has the uneasy sense that these unscheduled visitors are eating away at her time, but she doesn't know what to do about it. She tells herself that she *needs* to spend time with the art director; they stimulate ideas in each other, and do some of their best work when they're just hanging around chatting. When another writer drops in to blow off steam about a frustrating assignment, Sarah puts her work aside: "We writers have to stick together." And here's the creative director—her boss. He wants to ask about the script for Thursday's taping. She needs to finish the newspaper copy today, but he's her *boss*. So she'll just work harder after he leaves.

Josh is everyone's definition of a nice guy. Just look at all the helpful things he does for people. He agrees to coordinate the department's Christmas party. He's a member of the company's long-range planning task force. He has taken on a major responsibility at his children's school. And today a co-worker asked him to show her the new accounting software. All these extra duties mean Josh puts in long hours to get his own work done. But he likes helping other people out; besides, that's one way to get promoted, isn't it? And wouldn't his colleagues be offended if he said no?

Ego. Desire to please. Fear of offending. Fear of new challenges. Curiosity. Insecurity. Pride in your own abilities. Envy of others. Ambition. Perfectionism. These are all very human traits—and very deadly in your attempts to use your time efficiently and wisely. If you are going to gain control of your time, you must learn to recognize these powerful tendencies for what they are, and teach yourself to modify your actions. You may not be able to completely eradicate these traits, but you can get them under control.

I believe that this is the reason that the volumes of information we have seen in the last twenty years have been less than successful at solving our time problems: They generally focus on symptoms, rather than causes. Before you can correct a problem, you must understand it. As we move into Part Two, and start chipping away at the twenty biggest time wasters, you will see that we start by investigating the root causes of each problem, before we introduce the solutions. And often those causes are, in varying degrees, connected to simple human nature.

Whose Fault Is It?

One aspect of working on time management that is particularly difficult for some people is accepting the reality that they themselves are to blame for many of their time problems. It's another aspect of human nature: No one really *likes* to proclaim weaknesses. Instead we find it much easier to blame others. When people talk about their worst time problems, invariably they think in terms of the things in the work environment that are beyond their control—or that they *think* are beyond their control. There are many handy scapegoats, of course: drop-in visitors, meetings, inadequate equipment, people who fail to perform as expected, paperwork, inaccurate information, telephone interruptions, crises of one sort or other, many of which could have been anticipated and prevented.

Yet the true cause underlying most of these time wasters is found within the person who *allows* his or her time to be wasted. If you find that hard to believe, consider this example: The biggest single time waster, worldwide, is telephone interruptions. The person who has not thought about this will say, "But that's not *my* fault; these people are calling *me*." Yes, but you permit the interruption; you take the call. The question is, why? See if any of these apply:

_____ You don't want to be discourteous.
_____ You want to be considered an "available" manager.
_____ You assume the call will be significant, and therefore a legitimate interruption.
_____ You enjoy socializing.
_____ You like to stay informed about what's going on.
_____ You think you probably know the answer to the caller's question better than anyone else would.

So you see that that old devil, human nature, has led you into two traps: Because of ego, or other traits, you accept phone calls and allow yourself to be interrupted, and then you place blame for the interruption on the person who placed the call.

The real irony is that telephone interruptions are one of the *easiest* problems to solve. But first you have to see the problem in clear perspective.

I once conducted a time management seminar for a group of chief executives, and started off by asking them to list their biggest time wasters. These five items got the most mentions. Note that all are externally generated; the presidents are blaming others.

1. Incomplete information for solution
2. Employees with problems
3. Telephone
4. Routine tasks
5. Meetings

Part of the seminar included viewing a film that shows the president of a company in a normal working day, wasting time in many common ways. Later the seminar participants were asked if they could identify any new time wasters, and they produced this second list. You can see that these items are self-generated; the presidents, with their new insight, were now realizing the blame lay with themselves.

1. Attempting too much at once
2. Unrealistic time estimates
3. Procrastinating
4. Not listening
5. Not saying no

Old Habits, New Habits

Another reason many people have difficulty applying the techniques of good time management is that these techniques run counter to their personal habit patterns. Have you ever witnessed a situation like this? A colleague signs up for a workshop or class in time management techniques, comes back full of enthusiasm and determination, and then in about two weeks, he gradually starts slipping back into the old ways of doing things.

I have certainly witnessed it. In my years of teaching time management seminars, I have had many repeat customers. One man explained cheerily, "Well, I guess it just didn't take." This man's desire to make improvements was no match for the deeply ingrained habits of a lifetime. To make progress with time management, you have to look squarely at your own habits and be willing to do the work of changing them.

Habits are amazing. Few of us could explain rationally why we do certain things the way we do. We've been doing them that way for so long that we do them without thinking. If you doubt it, try this test. Which shoe do you put on first when you get dressed, right or left? Tomorrow, try the *other* one first. I did, and had the nagging feeling that something just wasn't right. I had the absurd urge to stop and take off my shoes and put the "correct" one on first.

When it comes to the pattern of how we use our time, habits can be particularly insidious. Sam reads his mail first thing in the morning; he's always done it that way. Alicia keeps two calendars, one for business appointments and one for her personal schedule; she started that practice on her very first job, when she received *two* appointment books as graduation gifts. Mary Beth has a well-established routine for correspondence. She writes her letters and interoffice memos in longhand on ruled tablets (claims she thinks better that way), has her assistant type up a draft, revises the draft, reviews the final copy for mistakes, and finally signs it.

Can you spot their mistakes? There is probably nothing in Sam's mail that can't wait till afternoon; he should put his first hour on his top-priority task. Mary Beth could cut her correspondence time down to one third if she would (1) let her assistant deal with routine correspondence and draft responses for noncritical situations, (2) learn the art of dictation, (3) give up the idea that every letter has to be 100 percent perfect, and (4) trust her assistant not to make mistakes. As for Alicia, even she acknowledges she frequently gets tangled up with overlapping commitments, but she ascribes this to her own carelessness, not seeing that her system is the real problem.

Unlearning old habits and learning new ones are difficult—and essential. Fortunately, there is an established process for teaching ourselves new habits, and it works. This process is described in detail in Part Three, for you will need it when you begin drawing up your action plan for change.

Interconnecting Threads

One other aspect of time management that makes it difficult for some people to be successful is that it is a complex process, made up of many elements that are interwoven. Sometimes we just don't know which thread to pull on. Even people with the best intentions can feel defeated because they don't know where to start.

Sorting out a situation and defining the real time wasters involved can be a bit overwhelming. In Part Two (Time Topic 5) you will picture yourself trapped in a conversation with an associate for "just a minute" and so be late for an important meeting. In just that one encounter are about a half-dozen mistakes in time management. When things are happening fast, we don't always see our situation clearly.

Stop now and take a quick look at the list of twenty time concerns at the start of Part Two. Notice the relationship between attempting too much and doing it yourself (that is, ineffective delegation). And doing it yourself, rather than delegating to a staff member, could be a result of believing your staff is inadequate. Another example: Someone who lacks the ability to say no will always be at the mercy of drop-in visitors, of telephone interruptions, of team members who are inclined to delegate upward, turning their problems over to the boss. And this: One identified time waster is lack of self-discipline. It is a clear problem of its own, and it is also interrelated with several others: failure to plan adequately, personal disorganization, and procrastination.

As you begin the process of getting your time habits under control, you may sometimes be frustrated by these multiple interconnections. Try not to let it bog you down. Over the years I have learned that if people develop an action plan and work at it regularly, focusing on what they think their difficulties are, things will fall into place. Here's the good news: Just as the problems are interrelated, so are the solutions. If you choose to focus, for instance, on developing self-discipline, you will almost automatically cure yourself of procrastination too.

Misconceptions About Time Management

Another part of the difficulty is that many of us are operating under misconceptions about what time management is and how it's supposed to work. See if any of these notions sound familiar to you.

• *Time management is nothing but common sense. I'm doing well at my job, so I must be managing my time just fine.* Maybe—but it's much more likely that you are successful *in spite of* your time management practices. What if I showed you how to double your productivity? How much *more* successful do you think you could be? And while it is true that almost all the solutions to time management problems are simple, what is not simple is the self-discipline to actually do them. As someone much smarter than me once said, common sense isn't all that common these days.

• *I work better under pressure; time management would take away that edge.* Nobody works better under pressure; what really happens is you do the best you can under the circumstances. Usually this is nothing but a subconscious rationale for procrastinating. If you put off a major task until the last minute, with the excuse that you work better under pressure, you leave yourself no time to do the planning that would produce superior results. You also leave no room for correcting mistakes, locating missing information, or incorporating better ideas that might come to you too late to be included. You get the job done, and you may feel like a hero, but the truth is that the work was just good enough, not "better." By not managing your time, you deny yourself the opportunity to do outstanding work.

• *I use an appointment calendar and a to-do list. Isn't that enough?* The way most people work with it, the to-do list can be a quagmire. The calendar tells you where you are today, but doesn't help much with next month, and it's almost impossible to retrieve something from the past. The best time management tool is an integrated system, one that allows you to retrieve information, track projects, focus on goals, and record key decisions.

• *People take time management too seriously; it takes all the fun out of life.* If constant stress, forgetting appointments, missing deadlines, and working until midnight are your idea of fun, you're welcome to it. Look at it this way: If you had two extra hours a day (and time management techniques can easily provide that), could you think of fun ways to spend those two hours?

• *Time management takes away your freedom—and I'm a spontaneous sort of person.* True freedom comes through discipline. Suppose you were suddenly offered an opportunity to stay at a friend's house in Key West for a week and you had to leave in two days. Are you organized enough to reschedule your work so you could go? That's freedom!

• *Time management might be good for some kinds of work, but my job is very creative. I can't be tied to a routine.* Time management is not fundamentally about routine; it's about self-discipline. Effective time management gives you time to be creative. It frees your mind of the worry and tedious detail that stand in the way of creative thinking.

• *The stuff they teach you in time management is a lot of work. I don't have time to do all that.* You don't have time *not* to. It's true that keeping a time log and writing a daily plan may be new to you, but they are not really time-consuming in themselves, once you learn how. A few minutes can save you hours.

There's a story about a man struggling to cut down enough trees to build a fence. An old farmer came by, watched for a while, then quietly said, "Saw's kinda dull, isn't it?"

"I reckon," said the fence builder.

"Hadn't ya better sharpen it?"

"Maybe later. I can't stop now—I got all these trees to cut down."

Time Management Is Self-Management

The idea of "time management" may be the biggest misconception of all. For time cannot be managed. At least not in the way other resources can.

Business is concerned with the wise management of five kinds of resources: capital, physical, human, information, and time. All of the first four can be manipulated in many directions. You can manage human resources: You can increase the size of your work force, or decrease it; you can change its composition, adding more of a certain specialty and subtracting others; you can move production workers off the line and retrain them in other functions. You can also manage capital. You can increase it, save it, spend it, or hold steady. You can invest it, put it into new production facilities, or fund a subsidiary. If you need more, you can sell shares in the company, get a loan, increase the price of your product.

But time, the invisible resource, is unique, because it is finite. There is only so much of it, and no matter what you do, you can't get more. The clock cannot be speeded up or slowed down. Time is the only resource that must be spent the instant it is received, and it must be spent at one fixed rate: sixty seconds per minute, sixty minutes per hour.

Thus, the very notion of time management is a misnomer. For we cannot manage time. We can only manage *ourselves* in relation to time. We cannot control how much time we have; we can only control how we use it. We cannot choose *whether* to spend it, but only how. Once we've wasted time, it's gone—and it cannot be replaced.

Two

New Perspectives: The Real Purpose of Time Management

Time, which once seemed free and elastic, has grown elusive and tight, and our measure of its worth is changing dramatically. In Florida a man bills his doctor $90 for keeping him waiting. In New York a woman pays someone $20 an hour to do her shopping . . . out of a catalog. For $1,500, you can have a fax machine put in your car, alongside your cellular phone, so people can reach you instantaneously with either printed or oral messages. Everyone, it seems, hands you a business card displaying a phone number, beeper number, fax number, and e-mail address.

What has all this gained us? Not more time. We already know there isn't any more. Not more freedom. If you pay someone to pick up your laundry while you stay late at the office, you're only trading one chore for another. Not more peace of mind. All around us we see frazzled parents, exhausted workers, families juggling multiple hectic schedules. As a nation, we seem to have run out of time.

My fear is that many people simply have missed the point about time management. Good time management techniques will save you at least an hour a day, probably two—but the real question is, what will you do with those extra two hours? Take on another project, and get frantic all over again?

The value of time management is not control of time per se, but the ways you can use time to improve your life. In this chapter, we discuss in detail these four important areas:

1. *Stress.* Managing time well can prevent much of the stress modern businesspeople are subject to.
2. *Balance.* Good time habits can enable us to achieve a more balanced life, with adequate time and energy for work, home, family, self.
3. *Productivity.* In the business world time equals productivity. If you can become more effective with your time, you automatically increase your productivity.
4. *Goals.* To make progress toward achieving your personal and professional goals, you need available time. Nothing can be done when you're out of time.

In all four areas, time is what makes success possible, but to my knowledge, time has not been linked directly with these key results areas before. That's why I sometimes refer to them as four "breakthrough" areas.

From this broadened perspective, we can see that the real value of time management is that it enhances our lives—in all dimensions. What we gain from time management, in essence, is not more time, but a better life.

Less Stress Through Time Control

We all know that running out of time puts us under stress. We try to get too much done in too little time. Decisions are made in haste and actions are taken under pressure. Planning is abandoned. Impulse replaces thought. Work hours lengthen as we struggle to get everything done. Effectiveness is diminished; deadlines are missed. Tension builds, tempers too; stress escalates. We all know about that kind of stress, right? What we may not know is how thoroughly time is connected to the problem.

Every thought, every action takes time. Everything that takes time has the potential of wasting time. If anything takes longer than it should, it has wasted time. If that wasted time puts you in jeopardy of running out of time on another obligation later in the day, you are suddenly facing great stress. So we can see that *every* time waster is a potential stressor.

This opens a new approach to managing stress. Rather than

allowing ourselves to be placed in positions of constant stress and then teaching ourselves coping techniques, we focus instead on managing our time more effectively. This way, we prevent most of the stress that time shortages inflict on us. So time management is stress management of the highest order.

This idea is so simple that it is easy to overlook. But think for a moment what it really means. Much has been written about stress management, particularly stress in the workplace and its cost to American business. Owners and chief executives are so concerned that they are taking serious and expensive remedial action: Bringing in outside consultants to teach classes and workshops in stress reduction techniques to all employees is one example; establishing on-site gyms and recreational facilities to let employees work off their tensions or underwriting memberships in community recreation centers is another.

On a more sober level, stress is directly linked to some of our most serious health concerns, particularly heart attacks and strokes. In the business world this takes a particularly dreadful toll, as companies are hit from two directions: rapidly rising costs of company-supported health care, and the shocking loss of promising young managers. Some workers have sued employers for "stress-induced disability" claims—and won.

How much better off would we be if we turned our energies toward *preventing* stress in the first place! Of course we'll never eliminate it totally. And of course not all stressors are time-related. But a very high percentage are, and they can be cured. Get rid of the situation that causes the stress, and you never have the stress. Simple, isn't it?

Balance Between Work and Personal Life

Are you a workaholic?
Is it really such a bad thing to be?

We've heard a lot about workaholics, not all of it bad. But is everyone talking about the same thing? Often when a word is coined to describe a phenomenon of interest, and when that phenomenon is widely discussed, it isn't long before the original definition starts to get fuzzy around the edges, and we soon discover that we have only a vague sense of what it really involves.

What is a workaholic, anyway? Consistently working long hours used to be considered the sign of workaholism. But today that perception is being challenged. All workaholics work long hours, but not everyone who works long hours is a workaholic. Many people put in long hours for other reasons—often because they simply have no choice. I know a remarkable young woman, a single mother with four young children, who holds down two jobs, one of them a very demanding, and very exhausting, nursing position. She works twelve-hour days five days a week, but is she a workaholic? She would not think so. "You do what you have to, that's all."

Other people work long hours for the simple reason that they don't know how to get their work done within regular hours. (They are the lucky ones—their workaholism is the easiest to cure.) And of course all of us put in long hours from time to time on big projects; we're really talking here about a chronic condition: working late every single night. Long hours can be a clue to help us recognize workaholism, but we must dig deeper and look for the reason behind the long hours.

Then there is the question of whether someone who really loves the work is a workaholic. "I really enjoy my work, so that's where I put most of my energy. What's wrong with that?" Nothing, as long as you reserve *some* energy for self and family. Liking your work is irrelevant to the issue of workaholism. This is true also of ambition: Working extra hard, which may mean working extra long, as part of your plan to advance in your field, is not workaholism, *as long as* you take care to provide some balance in other areas of your life.

And what about the really hard workers, the super-achievers? Are they workaholics? Not necessarily. Hard workers generally enjoy what they do and gain great satisfaction from the results. In fact, they are the ones sometimes referred to as "healthy" workaholics: They have high energy and a great zest for life; they tend to live longer, pile up more accomplishments, involve themselves in a wider range of activities, both professional and personal, and generally have a lot more fun.

The difference between simply working long hours (for

whatever reason) and workaholism is that workaholism is compulsive behavior, like alcoholism, drug dependency, gambling, or any other addiction. True workaholics are *addicted* to work. They have a compulsion to keep busy, and so they bury themselves in piles of paper. They gravitate toward work that is routine and time-consuming, with little consideration of whether the outcome is valuable to the company.

The underlying reasons behind the addiction may vary; workaholics might overindulge in work to escape from personal problems, to avoid going home to a troubled marriage, to boost their low self-esteem, or to enhance their feeling of being in control of their lives. But whatever the unconscious motivation, the end result is the same: inordinately long hours for the worker, great stress for the worker's family.

Are you a workaholic? That question, which I asked at the start of this section, is really a trick question. Denial is a strong characteristic of all forms of addictive behavior. So genuine workaholics never *think* they are. There are some clues. Dr. Marilyn Machlowitz, a management psychologist who has studied workaholics extensively, developed a test to measure the phenomenon; try this portion of her test for yourself.[1]

Take the Workaholic Test

1. Do you get up early, no matter how late you go to bed?
2. If you are eating lunch alone, do you read or work while you eat?
3. Do you find it difficult to do nothing?
4. Are you energetic and competitive?
5. Do you work on weekends and holidays?
6. Can you work any time and anywhere?
7. Do you find it hard to take a vacation?
8. Do you dread retirement?

If you answered yes to five or more questions, you may be a workaholic.

But is it really such a bad thing to be? This question is a bit more complex. Dr. Machlowitz defines a workaholic as "one whose desire to work long and hard is intrinsic and whose work habits almost always exceed the prescriptions of the job they do and the expectations of the people with whom and for whom they work."[2] Let's consider this for a moment. Exceeding your boss's expectations might or might not be a good thing; exceeding the prescriptions of your job seldom is.

Dr. Charles Garfield, professor of psychology at the University of California Medical School in San Francisco, has become known for his studies of peak performers, and his comments on workaholics are particularly relevant here. "Workaholics are addicted to work, not results," he says. "They work for work's sake and tend not to make a major impact. The workaholic never makes the discovery, writes the position paper, or becomes the chief executive officer."[3] Do workaholics contribute to the organization? Yes, says Garfield, because of the sheer volume of their work. But by the time they hit midcareer, their contributions become increasingly smothered by mountains of detail. In fact, many time management practices of workaholics are bizarre: (1) They tend to work the longest hours on the least productive tasks; (2) they tend to focus on the *visible* tasks over the number-one priority tasks; (3) they *refuse* to delegate when they can; *and* (4) they overreact to crises, plunging into a morass of frantic busyness which is frightening in its universality—even among managers and executives.

It is probably this aspect of the workaholic personality—this sense that their effectiveness is limited by their focus on minutiae—that has led to a gradual shift in thinking in executive offices around the country. Whereas once an employee who stayed late every night, took home a loaded briefcase, and came in on Saturdays to "clean up" would have been described as dedicated, loyal, and committed, today that person is looked on with suspicion. Senior managers observing this person know that, at the very least, the worker is disorganized; at worst, he or she is, through errors, bad judgment, or missed opportunities, actually causing harm to the company.

This shift in attitude is fairly recent, and not yet universal. There are still some who think "workaholic" is a compliment. Most enlightened business leaders, however, know better. They know that long hours produce fatigue, which produces mistakes. They know that the "hard-working" individual toiling late at night when the rest of the building is dark is probably working on the wrong kinds of things. They know that over-stuffed briefcases and desks piled with a jumble of files indicate not loyalty but poor delegation. They know that the clear, fresh, creative thinking that is the mark of the innovator is far more likely to come from a person who knows how to relax and refuel than from one who is mentally and emotionally exhausted.

When you work long hours, two things happen: You assume you have more time to get something done, so you slow your pace; and you get tired, so you can't work as briskly. For both reasons, you work less effectively and make mistakes, which leads to more long hours. It's not a crime to go home at 5 P.M.; organized people do it all the time. It's a sign of an efficient, productive worker.

So if you're working those long hours because you think your boss will be impressed, you are making a serious mistake, one with grievous consequences. For not only are you *not* making points with the boss, you are sacrificing one of your best sources of support for your professional ambitions: your family and loved ones—provided they're still around.

The toll on the families of workaholics is extreme. Divorces, failed relationships, alienated children with serious behavior problems—these are common in workaholic households. Even if we disregard for the moment the pain this addiction will inflict on your family, consider its boomerang effect. Sooner or later the turmoil at home will get to you, and will have a major impact on your effectiveness at work.

Have I convinced you that a workaholic is *not* a good thing to be? Good. Now, how do we get you out of it? Achieving balance between personal and professional life may be harder for some than others; some people may need professional counseling as they move through the process. But the fundamental cure is the same: Set goals that reflect a balance among various facets of your life, and learn to manage your time better.

Which brings us to the link between time and workaholism. Time gives us both the clue to recognize the problem (since all workaholics work long hours), and the key to the solution. If you study this book and really practice the principles of effective time management, you can learn to get the long hours under control. I believe this wholeheartedly, for I have witnessed it countless times.

And if you approach the process of goal setting, which is presented in the next chapter, from the perspective of achieving balance, you can be successful here as well. The key is to broaden your thinking: Goals should not focus exclusively on your professional life. You should also be setting goals that concern your spouse, children, and friends, your personal recreation, physical fitness, intellectual development, community involvement, and spiritual enrichment.

Personal Productivity

For many years American business and industry took worldwide economic supremacy for granted. Today, the economy is global and international competition is intense. U.S. businesses search for a critical competitive edge. Along the way, companies engage in serious and sometimes painful belt cinching. Terms like "cutback management," "downsizing," and "restructuring," are commonplace. In this environment, the importance of productivity is stressed. But what is productivity?

Productivity refers to the relationship between resources and results: What you put in, what you get out. It is often expressed as a formula:

$$\text{Productivity} = \text{Output} \div \text{Input}$$

The formula demonstrates that there are actually two ways of improving productivity: increasing output while holding input constant, or reducing input while holding output constant.

The value of this formula is that with it we can quickly measure degree of change. To see how it works, let's try some numbers.

If Wonderful Widget Works can produce 9,240 widgets (output) in 840 worker hours (input), the productivity level is 11; the workers can produce 11 widgets an hour. Wonderful Widget Works commits a certain level of resources—840 hours of production time—to produce a certain level of results, in this case a tangible product . . . 9,240 of them:

Productivity = 9,240 widgets [output] ÷ 840 hours [input] = 11

Now suppose that Wonderful Widget Works's main competition is taking away some of its customers. Management thinks it can gain its old customers back if it can cut the price of its widgets, which it can do if the manufacturing costs can be reduced. To affect manufacturing cost, management has two angles of attack: [A] somehow get its workers to produce more widgets per hour (increase output, hold input constant), or [B] reduce the number of workers and train people to work more efficiently so that they produce the same number of widgets as the larger crew (decrease input, hold output steady). Here's how the two approaches are expressed in the formula:

[A] Productivity = 10,080 widgets ÷ 840 hours = 12

[B] Productivity = 9,240 widgets ÷ 770 hours = 12

Now, Wonderful Widget Works could really run circles [C] around the competition if it improves *both* sides of the productivity formula, making it possible for a smaller work force to produce even *more than* the larger work force had:

[C] Productivity = 11,088 widgets ÷ 770 hours = 14.4

Maybe you think that 14.4 widgets per hour isn't all that much better than 11 widgets per hour, given the world's currently diminished appetite for widgets. But suppose they were computer chips, or cars? Which, of course, they are. The admittedly oversimplified widget story is really an allegory for modern industrial progress.

You have probably already recognized productivity as the instrument by which Japanese industry made such phenomenal gains. When we in America first compared ourselves to the Japanese, we had reason to be disturbed. They were bettering our performance in both arms of the productivity formula. The quality of their products (output) far exceeded ours, and the cost of their input was notably lower. The Japanese auto industry, for instance, claims to have only five levels of management, compared with eleven for American auto makers.

Where does time fit into the picture? The input part of the formula, remember, is all the resources (including time, the invisible resource) invested in producing the output. The output part of the formula is "captured" time, time in the form of results. In both A and B scenarios, Wonderful Widget Works was actually manipulating time when it managed to get its workers to make widgets faster. Modern time management techniques hold the prospect of improving *both* sides of the formula: doing more (increased output) in less time (decreased input).

The fact of the matter is that a larger portion of the work of American business is now conducted in offices than on production lines. These days we make more memos, more marketing plans, more financial projections, than widgets. Therefore our productivity focus must shift to individuals. If the memo writers, the marketing vice-presidents, and the finance officers can learn to get better results in whatever they undertake, and do it in less time, the impact on the U.S. economy could be powerful.

There is much that can be done. Industrial psychologists have long held that managers, on the average, were doing some things less productively than they might—70 percent less. While little research has been done in this area, there are some data to support the view that the average manager is only 30 percent effective. Personally, my years as an observer of American business have thoroughly convinced me that it is true: Most of us work at about one-third effectiveness most of the time.

For example, my surveys show that managers typically spend six minutes per telephone call; most of them, when reviewing detailed time logs, conclude that they could have covered the important points in two minutes. Even if all they could accomplish is cut the time in half, to three minutes, with comparable results, their productivity has doubled and a scarce resource—time—has been saved.

Have you ever noticed that on your last work day just before going away on vacation, you get three days' work done? Do you need any more evidence that most people work at about one-third efficiency most of the time? Of course no one expects you to work at peak capacity 100 percent of the time. But if all you did was work at two-thirds capacity, you'd immediately increase your output to twice what it is now. You'd be getting two days' work done in one day!

A remarkable example of increased productivity occurred in the management offices of a Canadian airline. The president was in the habit of holding daily staff meetings, each one and a half hours long, without any agenda. No wonder all ten of his top managers named "meetings!" as their top time waster. After learning some better meeting techniques, the president switched the format. Staff meetings would be held only once a week, not every day; they would be limited to one hour, and they would always be run by agenda. Right away the time investment dropped dramatically, from a total of seven and a half hours a week to one hour. After six months, when all had learned how to use the agenda for the powerful tool it is, they had also *doubled* the results gained from the meetings. So the total productivity of the staff meeting increased fifteenfold.

Original productivity   = 100 [base results] ÷ 7.5 hours = 13
Improved productivity   = 200 [doubled results] ÷ 1 hour = 200
              200 ÷ 13   = 15.38
Degree of improvement = 1538 %

Here's another example from the health care industry. A hospital administrator and the members of the top team discovered, after keeping a time log for a week, that they were wasting nearly two hours a day because of an "open door" policy. They interrupted each other at will whenever an idea hit any one of them. After attending a time management seminar they redefined "open door" to mean "accessible" and closed the doors to provide time for concentrated, uninterrupted work. They set regular times to meet with each other to cover questions that had arisen in the interim.

Immediately, the "lost" hours dropped from two to less than half an hour, so that in a normal eight-hour day they had seven and a half "real" work hours, instead of six. Furthermore, they estimated that in each of those more focused hours, they accomplished 50 percent *more* than they had in the old interruption-plagued hours.

This is another valuable way to think about time management. Once you realize that you can quantify it, and measure its effect on productivity, you can clearly see the benefit of learning to use your time more effectively. Thus the emphasis shifts subtly from time management for its own sake, to increased productivity.

Most of this book shows you how to get rid of the biggest time wasters in your life. With this broader perspective, learn to see time wasters as productivity targets. To sharpen your view, set some actual targets.

One group of senior managers I worked with did exactly that. They discovered the five time wasters that were giving them the most trouble, and measured the amount of time wasted. Then they established quantified goals for improvement, and chose the techniques for achieving improvement and the tools they would use to measure improved results. Although your personal time wasters may be different, you can adapt their process to your own situation. To get you started, here is their plan for the first two time wasters.

1. *Management by crisis*: By anticipating crises and taking steps to prevent them, reduce by half the time now spent reacting to crises, while maintaining comparable results (100 percent). Productivity Improvement target: 200.

$$\text{Productivity [P]} = \text{Results [R]} \div \text{Time [T]}$$
$$= 100 \div .5 = 200$$

2. *Telephone interruptions*: Through specific control measures, decrease the time lost by telephone interruptions down to one quarter (25 percent). After learning how to be more efficient with calls, target an increase of 50 percent in results achieved. Total Productivity Improvement target: 600.

$$P = R \div T = (150 \div .25) = 600$$

In the competitive environment in which all businesses now operate, it is not at all unusual to hear this sort of complaint:

"We just had a 10 percent cutback in personnel, yet we're expected to *increase* our production. How on earth can we do that?" We have just seen one very important solution: better time management. Anyone who makes a serious effort can save two hours a day. That's ten hours a week, forty hours a month. So every month you get an extra week, twelve extra weeks a year. That's the same as having three months' extra work time a year per person. Imagine what your organization could accomplish if everyone in it had fifteen months available each calendar year!

Success in Achieving Goals

"If you don't know where you're going, it doesn't matter which road you take." To that familiar adage, I would add: "And it doesn't matter how long it takes you to get there."

Without goals, your course through life will be haphazard, careless, and ineffective. Without time, even the simplest goals cannot be achieved. This linkage of time management with success in achieving your goals provides our fourth breakthrough area. Here again we have clear evidence that the careful husbandry of the resource that is time provides rich results.

Goals are one way—and a very powerful way—to motivate yourself to greater accomplishments. But no one ever met a demanding goal without devoting time to it. Making sure you have the time to devote to your goals is the role of time management.

Over the years I have seen many salespeople achieve phenomenal results from setting goals that were very demanding, often beyond anything they considered possible. Most of them tell me that the key that makes everything possible is gaining control of their time management, so they are free to concentrate on their sales goals. One financial consultant gave me a remarkable demonstration. He set *two* demanding goals: within two years, double both his income *and* vacation time with his family. In the first year his earnings rose from $80,000 to $120,000 and his vacation time from two weeks to four. The second year he reached his income goal of $160,000, and took *six* weeks' vacation. If you could ask him how he did it, he'd say time management.

So, you need time to meet your goals. But a complementary force is also at work: *Setting goals will give you more time.*

Human nature being what it is, if we have no particular objective to accomplish on a given day, we tend to meander around rather aimlessly. On the other hand, if we have several key objectives, and we consider them truly significant—and if we know a few basic principles of time management—we can accomplish an enormous amount in that same day. The key is concentration of effort on your real priorities. Having goals around which to focus your day's activities provides the structure for successfully accomplishing them through better time management.

People who have the most difficulty with time are often those with no clear goals. If they don't have goals, they really don't have a problem with time because they aren't going anywhere anyway. If they do have goals, they need control over time so they can accomplish them. You need time to achieve goals. You need goals to make serious gains in time management. This symbiotic connection is so critical to your success in time management that it deserves a full treatment of its own, and is discussed in the next chapter.

The Real Purpose of Time Management

I promised you at the beginning of this chapter that with good time management you could save yourself two hours a day. But now I'll ask you again the question I asked you then: What are you going to do with those two hours? The gains that you can create by managing time are pointless unless you have a plan for using them to some purpose.

A man I know bought a home in a rural section of Pennsylvania a few years back; there were several cherry trees on the property, and he thoroughly enjoyed the fruit the first summer. Then he became interested in seeing if he could improve on things and did some reading over the winter. He's a thorough sort of fellow, and so by the next year, he had doubled his cherry crop. But he hadn't thought about what he would do with all those cherries, and most of them rotted on the ground. (Actually, it wasn't a total loss; the neighborhood birds had a feast.)

Time management is not about time in the abstract; it's about what we can accomplish with time. In this chapter, we have looked with new eyes at some of the ways better time management can enhance your life. When you learn to use effectively the time that is given to you, you can have more time with your family, avoid getting stressed out, improve your personal level of productivity, and be more successful in achieving your goals.

Getting control of your time means facing up to the fact that *you* are usually the problem, not someone else. It means doing the hard work of changing well-established habits. It means holding your ground against the negative tugs of human nature. It's not easy. However, it is definitely worth the effort, for the benefits are profound.

Notes

1. Marilyn Machlowitz, *Workaholics: Living With Them, Working With Them* (Reading, Mass.: Addison-Wesley, 1980), pp. 17–20. Reprinted by permission of the author.
2. Machlowitz, *Workaholics*, p. 137.
3. Charles Garfield quoted in "Why Workaholics Work," *Newsweek*, April 27, 1981.

Three

Planning Puts You in Control

It's 7:30 in the morning. Paul Barrington has arrived at work early because he wants extra time to work on his proposal. He gets on the elevator with Chris, the government relations specialist; she asks if she can meet with him some time today to gather more material for her presentation to the legislature's subcommittee on housing. Mentally flipping through his calendar, Paul suggests 10:30. Out of the elevator, Paul decides to see if the fax from Australia arrived during the night. He passes by the lounge and stops in for a cup of coffee to take back to his desk to "get him going"; while there, he gets ensnared in a discussion about the mayor's press conference yesterday. Striding down the hall to his office, Paul runs into a section head from another department, who asks if Paul can help him locate that computer consultant Paul used three years ago. "Sure," Paul says, "call me later. But, you know, wait a second. There's something you should know about him. . . ."

When he finally gets near his office, Paul sees his assistant frantically waving at him. Paul's boss has called for him three times already this morning, and now he's *really* anxious for Paul to come up there. As it turns out, the matter isn't all that urgent, but Paul takes advantage of the opportunity to talk over another situation with the boss. All told, it's an hour and a half before Paul returns to his own office. His plans to work on his proposal have to wait a while, for the phone calls have been stacking up. He starts returning the calls, but many of those people are not in now, so he leaves messages. And he forgets all about the 10:30 meeting with Chris, and has to reschedule for the afternoon.

After lunch, Paul makes a valiant attempt to get through the morning's mail. He doesn't quite finish, though, for Howard drops by to ask what he should do about the Harriston Grain project. When Chris comes in, he tries to answer her questions while looking through his cluttered desk for the files he needs. Then he has to cut the meeting short because his assistant comes in to say he's been asked to attend the meeting of the president's task force. When that meeting finally winds down, Paul puts in another hour or so returning phone calls to people who returned *his* calls, and finally gives up. An exhausted Paul heads home around 6:00, wondering where the day went, and whether he'll have a chance tomorrow to draft his proposal.

Paul's problem is that he has allowed other people to run his day for him. With no clear plan for the day, he is forever at the mercy of the last thing that clamors for his attention—or the loudest.

In this chapter we apply the idea of planning—one major function of management—to time. *Planning* your day, rather than allowing it to unfold at the whim of others, is the single most important piece in the time management puzzle. In a nutshell, this is the process.

1. Set long-range goals and the objectives linked to them.
2. Establish priorities among those goals and objectives based on their long-range importance and short-range urgency.
3. Learn your personal energy cycle and sketch out an "ideal day" based on your best working times.
4. From these three building blocks—goals, priorities, ideal day—create a plan for the day and *write it down*.

Nothing that you do in your attempts to better manage your time will be more valuable than this written plan. Without it, you are totally at the mercy of other people's demands on your time. With it, you always know where you are and where you should be, and, equally important, you know what to do with new things that come along during the day—as they inevitably will.

Goals

If you're like most people, the idea of goals makes you faintly uncomfortable. It's the same vague guilt you associate with New Year's resolutions. You make them because you think you should; it's somehow expected. But experience has taught you that those resolutions tend to fall apart sooner or later (usually sooner), and so your efforts at making them are halfhearted—at best.

We do the same thing with goals—if we do anything at all. "Be successful in my job." "Provide for my children's education." A half-hearted goal *may* get you halfway to where you want to go . . . but I doubt it. It's more likely to get you just as far as the first detour, and off you go in another direction.

Why does the notion of setting goals seem threatening? Fear of failure. (If I set this goal, I'm committing myself. What if I can't accomplish it?) Fear of success, maybe. Uncertainty over how to go about it. Fear of the unknown. Anxiety about the riskiness of it all. Those are all very common feelings. But don't let them stop you. Just as you did with other qualities of human nature that tend to interfere with success, acknowledge the situation, recognize your feelings—and then get on with things.

Setting goals for significant accomplishments you want to achieve in your life, both personal and professional accomplishments, costs you nothing. *Failure* to set them can cost you plenty. You are smack in the middle of the only life you're going to have. You can choose to succeed, or choose to drift; having goals makes the difference.

The Company's Goals

Some of your goal planning involves achievements that are important to you as an individual (whether personal or professional). Other goals are dictated by, or related to, the organization's strategic plans and, in turn, your boss's plans and priorities for you and other team members.

In a perfect world, the organization's long-range goals would be made known to all employees, and all bosses would use those corporate goals to set the department's priorities and clearly communicate those priorities to everyone. In the real world, that doesn't always happen. If your boss does not seem to have clear objectives on which to base the priorities for assigning your work, you must take action. Ask for an appointment, and make your case like this:

"I know you have told me that I'm doing just fine, and I appreciate your confidence, but the truth is, I'm starting to feel uneasy about something. I'm not always sure that I'm working on the right things, on the things you'd want me to be working on. I think that's probably the reason I have to interrupt you so much, to get your assessment on what's the most important thing for me to be doing on any given day.

"I think I have an answer. I've written down what I think are the most important goals for me for the next three months, with a deadline for each one. If you'll approve them I won't have to keep bothering you to okay the things I'm doing. I think I'll get more done for you, and we'll both know that it will be the things you think are the most important. So if you wouldn't mind okaying this, I'll stop by tomorrow before the staff meeting and pick it up."

If you don't get a positive response right away, keep at it until you do. It is the most important job insurance policy you'll ever have. When the edict comes down to "cut all personnel back 10 percent," the last to be cut will be those who can point to specific accomplishments. If they weren't written down, don't expect any boss to remember them.

A Goal-Setting Process

A few years ago, on a combined business and pleasure trip in the Southeast, my wife and I met two young people on two different occasions. They were about the same age, in their mid-twenties, but very different in other ways. Our conversations were rather brief, the sort of chance encounter you have when you're traveling, but they showed me something vital about goals.

One was our waitress in a dinner house; her accent was

obviously European, and we quickly learned that she was from Germany. I asked why she had come to the United States.

"I want to own my own business in five years, and I've decided an MBA will help me be successful at it."

"So you're in graduate school now?"

"No, I'm taking some math and business classes at the university here. I need to do that before I can get into graduate school, and I have just one semester to go."

"But why are you waiting tables full time?"

"To earn the money for my last semester."

Our second encounter was with a young man working at the service station where we bought gas. His way of talking seemed to indicate an educated mind, and so out of curiosity I asked him about himself. He was indeed educated—a college graduate who had done the course work for a master's degree, but not completed the thesis. When I asked what he wanted to do with his life, he answered, "Build a cabin in the woods and be close to nature." Had he ever lived alone, in a solitary setting? No. Had he ever built anything before? No. Well, did he have the financial resources to hire someone to build it for him? No. Did he own any land? No. Did he have a plan for how he was going to go about getting his cabin? No.

Both these two young people had goals, but which do you think has the better chance of achieving the goal? My money's on the waitress. She is a good example of how the goals process should work: Start with a long-range goal, then work backward. The young man, in contrast, shows us how *not* to do it. In effect, he's saying, "I have a dream, but I'm doing nothing to turn it into reality. I'm just taking things one day at a time. I'll see where it gets me, and then I'll go from there." We've already seen where it got him, and it's pretty clear where he's going.

The goal-setting sequence starts with the long-range goal, a specific target: "To have my own business in five years." Then work carefully down from the long range all the way to today, setting successively shorter-range targets, usually called objectives. In other words, set a large goal and then break it down into smaller, more doable pieces—advice you've probably heard before. A significant goal can seem overwhelming, way off in the distance. A short-range objective seems more possible; therefore, we're not afraid to tackle it. And that means we are much more likely to be successful with the larger goal. Let's take a look at two examples of this process, one involving a personal goal and one a professional goal.

1. *Planning a personal goal.* You are interested in community affairs and have decided you'd like to become an officer in a particular civic organization that you respect. Reviewing your strengths, you conclude that the position of development officer is the best use of your talents, and that a three-year time frame is reasonable. You target becoming chair of the fund-raising committee within two years, and doing the best job of fund raising the organization has ever seen. By the end of this year, you plan to have served as a member of the existing fund-raising committee, and done an outstanding job. This week you will phone the current chair of the committee and volunteer your services for the annual auction. Tomorrow and the next day you will contact previous auction organizers and set times to visit with them and gather ideas. Today you will phone the office of the organization and collect the necessary names and phone numbers. Note that you started with one specific goal: become development officer in three years. Without that long-range goal, none of the other decisions would have made sense.

2. *Planning a professional goal.* As part of its long-range plan, your company has announced that it will establish a new division in three years. You would like to become manager of the information services department for the new division. You know there will be stiff competition from others in the company. You have been a section manager in your current division a little less than a year; a move up to department manager would be considered a significant promotion in a relatively short period—not unheard of in your organization, but unusual. You will need an aggressive plan.

As one part of your plan you establish objectives tied to the company's formalized educational standards for management-level positions. You decide that within two years you will obtain the education necessary to fulfill the requirements for department manager. In one year you will be promoted to assistant department manager. To do that you will fulfill the educational requirements for assistant department manager within six months. By the end of this week you will ask the personnel director to advise you on achieving these objectives and to identify courses that might be helpful. Today you will call the personnel director to make the appointment.

What Do Goals Look Like?

Many people use the terms "goal" and "objective" interchangeably. Technically they are not the same. A goal is long range; the period of time varies considerably, by profession, industry, and individual situation. Since it may take fifty years to grow a tree, long-range planning in the lumber industry will be quite different from most. Objectives are the intermediate targets with shorter time frames. The two examples above started with a goal and worked through staged objectives.

Here's a definition that works for both: a goal, and an objective, is a predetermined end result. *Predetermined.* You don't shoot first and then call whatever you hit the target. For example, your objective or goal might be improving the productivity of your section by 15 percent in six months; getting six new accounts for the firm by year-end; increasing your income 30 percent next year; being promoted to general manager by a certain date; taking a European vacation with your family two summers from now; buying your own home within three years.

There are certain attributes that effective goals must have.

- *A goal must be demanding.* This is the most important quality of all. A goal that is demanding motivates us to do our best. In a time management seminar not long ago, we had one participant, a salesman, who had never taken goal setting seriously. His previous year's sales were $12.3 million, and his goal for the coming year was $13 million—not much of a rise. After the discussion on goals in the seminar that day, he decided to up his next year's goal to $15 million. Six months later, he called to let me know his success: He was doing so well he had changed his goal to $17 million. "And if things keep on this way, I might even hit $20 million."

"In that case," I said, "why isn't your goal $20 million?"
Don't make your goals too easy; you'll be cheating yourself.

• *A goal must be achievable.* On the other hand, don't make your goals unrealistically high. You'll only frustrate yourself, and you may give up. Goals that are clearly unattainable destroy morale and kill motivation.

• *A goal should be specific and measurable.* If your goal is vague and unspecific, how will you know when you have achieved it? "To delegate more" is not a measurable goal; how much and what, specifically, will you delegate, and to whom, and when? "Spend more time with my family" is not an adequate goal. Compare this: "Home in time for supper with the kids four nights during the week; no work on Saturday after 12:00; one weekend excursion with the whole family every month." With specific goals like this you have something concrete to shoot for, and you have a way to know if you succeeded.

• *A goal must have a deadline.* Otherwise, it will not be taken seriously. Deadlines perform an extremely important function in goal setting: They provide a sense of urgency and a way of tracking progress. Both these elements greatly increase the probability that the goal will be achieved. A goal without a deadline is a dream.

• *A goal should be agreed to by those who must achieve it.* If those who will be responsible for reaching a target are involved in setting it, they will feel an enthusiasm for the goal and a strong commitment to reaching it. After all, who wants to see his or her own goals fail? Without this participation, this sense of ownership, the best you can hope for is effort made from obligation rather than commitment.

• *A goal should be written down.* If it is not, it is too easily forgotten. If you try to retain it in your mind, it may change every time you think about it. All serious goal setters not only write down their goals but keep them visible so they will be reminded of them periodically.

• *A goal should be flexible.* If conditions that affect your goal should change, for reasons outside your control, you should re-examine your goal. Don't cling stubbornly to something that is no longer possible. The situation may call for either an upward or a downward adjustment. One caution: Don't be too quick to lower your goals if the outside environment changes negatively; it may be that by working smarter you can offset the downward effect.

Time and Goals

Establishing specific goals is the first step in effective time management. This is absolutely critical, and it is often overlooked. As you will see, your plan for the day, that marvelous tool that makes time your partner rather than your enemy, starts with your goals. For now, remember this key point: You should organize your days so that you are, to the greatest degree possible, spending your time on activities that will help you reach your goals.

As you make progress in your efforts to control time, you will want to set goals for the time you save. I think you will like the results.

Your goals set the focus for how you spend your time. And, it bears repeating, there is a tremendous reciprocal effect as well. As you become more adept at using your time effectively, you find that you make greater progress toward your goals. Which gives you greater incentive to bring your goals to the forefront, perhaps raising your sights even higher.

Priorities

People often confuse goals, or objectives, with priorities. Quite simply, priorities are objectives that have been ranked in order of importance. Take your objectives, stand them on end, and whatever is on top is your number-one priority. The next one down is the number-two priority, and so on.

Recently, someone protested, "But all I *have* are priorities! I'm swimming in priorities and I don't know where to start." My answer: They may all be priorities, but they're not all *number-one* priorities. With a little practice, you can learn to discriminate among them.

The concept of priority has two aspects: long-range importance, and short-range urgency. A task with long-range importance is one that you could look back on at the end of, say, a year, and know that it was vital that you spent time on it. If your public relations agency has one major client and five much smaller ones, work connected to developing the communications plan for the large client has a high long-range importance. Short-range urgency refers to tasks that, regardless of how important they may be, *have* to be done at once. Today is the day to register for summer camp; going to camp may not be of significant long-range importance (although your daughter probably will disagree), but the task, if it is to be done, must be done today.

Priority Matrix

Both aspects of priority have varying degrees. Some things are only moderately significant in terms of long-range importance; some are just "sort of" urgent. Some chores are neither long-range important nor short-range urgent; some are both. It is possible to quantify these different degrees of both aspects, combine the numbers, and thus establish an overall ranking for your tasks. In the system I use, items that are of highest importance, or greatest urgency, are assigned a 1; medium importance or urgency earns a 2; and lower importance or urgency gets a 3. Let's see how it works.

Suppose you are the marketing coordinator in a medium-size architecture/engineering firm. It's Thursday afternoon and you're leaving for vacation at the end of the business day tomorrow. Between now and then, you have these five tasks to complete.

1. Sort slides of bank project.
2. Check audiovisual equipment for next week's new-business presentation.
3. Conduct training session on presentation techniques with new engineer.

4. Review PUD (public utility district) substation proposal and deliver by deadline.
5. Meet with graphic designer on new logo.

Analyze each one in turn. The bank slides are primarily for the slide library; they probably won't be needed soon. Importance, 3; urgency, 3. The new-business presentation is very important; your firm has made it through the first two cuts, and the project is a big one. Importance, 1; urgency, 1. The new engineer probably won't be involved in next week's presentation, but still needs to be oriented. Importance, 2; urgency, 3. The utility district has called for companies to submit proposals if they wish to be considered for architectural services on the new substation; you think your firm's chances of being selected are slight, but the proposal deadline is 4 P.M. Friday. Importance, 3; urgency, 1. The designer has some rough sketches of the logo to show you; she'd like your reaction so she can go forward while you're away. Importance, 2, urgency 1.

Now add up the numbers, using a Priority Matrix like the one shown in Figure 1, and see how the jobs stack up. As it turns out, the first item on your original to-do list is actually the lowest priority. So you will plan to work on it last. If some new task arises needing your attention, you may not even get to the slide sorting at all. But because this last item is also your lowest-priority item, it will not be so critical if it has to slip until after the vacation.

Obviously you are not going to make up a priority matrix every day, filling in items and adding up numbers. Most of the time you do this analytical process in a more intuitive fashion, often quite rapidly. I developed the matrix to demonstrate that priorities are relative, and that they should be set systematically rather than haphazardly. If you practice the procedure a few times, you will soon master the technique and be able to put it to good use in your own planning.

Priorities and Time

A little later on in this chapter you will see how goals, objectives, and priorities all fit together in the planning process that culmi-

Figure 1. Sample priority matrix.

Task	Long-range Importance	Short-range Urgency	Weight	Priority
1. bank slides	3	3	6	5
2. a-v equipment	1	1	2	1
3. training	2	3	5	4
4. PUD proposal	3	1	4	3
5. logo	2	1	3	2

nates in a written daily plan. At the moment I want to show you just how powerful an understanding of priorities can be.

A manager in a technical services consulting firm, with a firm grounding in the concept of priorities, had ranked her major tasks for the day in order of importance:

1. New product proposal
2. Performance appraisals
3. Staff meeting
4. Back correspondence

Then, using a time log (which you will learn about in the next chapter), she recorded how much time she actually devoted to those four jobs during the day.

New product proposal	10%
Performance appraisals	20%
Staff meeting	35%
Correspondence	35%

The job with the highest priority received the least amount of attention!

This, I think, is one of the key values of priorities. They guide you in planning your day; they tell you where you should be putting your most serious energy.

The following story is a classic, but so important, it deserves to be retold so that old and new readers alike can reap its benefit.

When Charles Schwab was president of Bethlehem Steel, he confronted Ivy Lee, a management consultant, with an unusual challenge. "Show me a way to get more things done," he demanded. "If it works, I'll pay you anything within reason."

Lee handed Schwab a piece of paper. "Write down the things you have to do tomorrow." When Schwab had completed the list, Lee said, "Now number these items in the order of their real importance." Schwab did, and Lee said, "The first thing tomorrow morning, start working on number one and stay with it until it's completed. Then take number two, and don't go any further until it's finished or until you've done as much with it as you can. Then proceed to number three, and so on. If you can't complete everything on schedule, don't worry. At least you will have taken care of the most important things before getting distracted by items of less importance.

"The secret is to do this daily. Evaluate the relative importance of the things you have to get done, establish priorities, record your plan of action, and stick to it. Do this every working day. After you have convinced yourself that this system has value, have your people try it. Test it as long as you like, and then send me a check for whatever you think the idea is worth."

In a few weeks, Schwab mailed Lee a check for $25,000. He later said this was the most profitable lesson he'd learned in his entire business career.

If you take nothing else away from this book, remember the following highly important principle: Identify your number-one priority and get it done first!

The Ideal Day

You may think that your job is so filled with interruptions, crises, and unusual problems that you have no such thing as a "typical" day. Yet all of us have significant tasks that occur more or less regularly. Teachers have to make up lesson plans. Department managers must confer regularly with section managers. Public relations consultants develop communication campaigns for their clients. Finance officers prepare quarterly reports for the SEC. And some elements of those tasks may be done every day: The publicist writes a press release every day during the campaign, the finance manager reviews figures from one department each day in preparation for the report. And every day there are phone calls to make and correspondence to answer.

Who decides *when* you do these things, at what hour of the day? You do.

Now add to that the idea of your personal energy cycle. Most of us have certain times of the day when we're more energetic, mentally fresher, and other times when we're less effective. Many people have an energy "dip" right after lunch, for instance, or get a second wind around 4:00. Study yourself for a few days. Are you a slow starter, or do you do your best work first thing in the morning? Plot your own energy cycle, and plan your day around it. Schedule your key tasks for your best working times, and work on those tasks at the same time each day.

The ideal day is a template, in effect, for your daily plan. It indicates blocks of time for major categories of activities. Then, for each day's plan, you schedule the specifics in those major categories. Here's how Frank Sullivan, former president and CEO of a large insurance company, did it. He devoted much of his day to appointments with those in the company who needed to confer with him.

Frank Sullivan's Ideal Day

6:00–6:30	Commute and dictate
6:30–7:00	Mass
7:00–8:00	Quiet hour, organize
8:00–8:30	Meet with administrative assistant
8:30–9:00	Review mail
9:00–11:00	Scheduled appointments
11:00–12:00	Phone
12:00–2:00	When possible, use time as follows:
	12:00–1:00 lunch with VPs
	1:00–2:00 staff appointment, *Or*
	12:00–2:00 outside luncheon
2:00–3:30	Scheduled appointments
3:30–4:00	Sign dictation, review mail, etc.
4:00–5:00	Phone

Note: Try to keep Fridays clear for planning, emergencies, and catch-up.

This notion of the ideal day is an extremely powerful time management tool. If this approach is new for you, you will need to practice a bit in order to fully incorporate it into your planning. Note that the first step is to list the major categories that come up regularly in your job, then establish time blocks in which to slot them.

Sitting quietly in Frank Sullivan's ideal day is another very valuable tool: the quiet hour (7:00–8:00). This is covered thoroughly in Part Two (Time Topic 3), but for now the important thing to note is that the quiet hour is included in the schedule; it has its own time block, to guarantee that it happens.

Putting It All Together

Let's review. Because you want to do things with your life, rather than merely drift along, you have set long-range goals in both the personal and professional arenas. Then, working backward, you have planned successively shorter-range objectives that are tied to the goals. Each objective is a specific target with a deadline; taken one at a time, they lead you toward your goal.

Next, you have learned the concept of priorities, and practiced a technique for ranking activities in priority order by assigning numeric weights to them. These two building blocks work hand in hand as a foundation for planning your time: Set goals and objectives, rank them in priority order, make a time plan based on them.

The third building block of the plan is what we have called your ideal day: your "base sheet" for the daily plan, with blocks of time allocated to key task categories. Your personal ideal day will be different from someone else's, because it reflects your own energy cycle. This guarantees that you will do your priority tasks at your peak hours.

The thinking process follows this sequence:

1. *Start* with long-range goals and objectives.
2. *Relate* the day's activities to those goals.
3. *Assign* priorities to the day's tasks according to their contribution to your overall goals.
4. *Schedule* tasks according to priority and to the degree of concentration required.
5. *Stay on track,* using the plan to guide you through crises and interruptions.

Larry Appley, former president of the American Management Association, summed things up nicely: "When all is said and done, it's a question of knowing where you want to go, planning the best way to get there, and controlling events to conform to the plan."

The system I find most useful has the entire week visible. Each day of the week is divided into three sections titled Goals, Appointments, and To Do. Using the "ideal day" template, you block out in the appointments section times designated for major activities. In addition, of course, you record meetings, call-backs, appointments, and status checkpoints on projects at the appropriate times. Exactly how you choose to write up your plan, in which format, and in which kind of physical calendar system are less important than the fact that you do it.

If you sincerely want to make more effective use of your time, planning in advance is the best thing you can do for yourself. A daily plan, in writing, is *the single* most effective time management strategy, yet not one person in ten does it. The other nine will always go home muttering to themselves. "Where did the day go?"

Four

Making Changes:
Start Where You Are

"I just don't know where the time goes."

Then it's time you found out. Time doesn't mysteriously evaporate; it "goes" where you tell it to, or permit it to wander, or allow other people to yank it. If you don't know where it goes, how can you control it?

Take a moment now and look at the start of Part Two, where the twenty time wasters are listed. Chances are, you have experienced all of them at one time or another. But no doubt some represent more of a problem for you than others. If you are to improve your effective management of time—which is the fundamental goal of this book—you must determine which of the time wasters are your most serious concerns, and get to work on them. A problem that has not been identified cannot be corrected.

To pinpoint those time concerns, you must first take note of how you spend your days. To use your time more effectively, the essential first step is to discover what you currently do with it. The only adequate tool for doing that is a time log, a detailed record of all the things that you turn your attention to during a work day.

Right about here a lot of people tend to balk. "Ah," they say, "I think I can skip that part; I already know pretty much what I do in any given day." Well, if I had bet a dollar with everybody who's ever said that to me, I could have retired long ago. The fact is, *no one* has a realistic idea of where their time goes without a time log. People are *always* surprised.

Our minds have a way of playing tricks on us. We tend to forget about the small interruptions—not realizing how much time they eat up in the aggregate. We somehow overlook the time spent socializing: "It's not that important." We're not aware of how much of our total time goes to activities that produce zero results—like looking for a file and not finding it, or calling someone who is not at her desk—because each one seems minor when it is happening. But when we add them all up, we see with dazzling clarity just how much time we waste every day. A time log confronts you with the reality of what you do with your time.

Another common complaint about time logs is that it takes too much time to do them. If you think you're far too busy to keep a time log, you are, *ipso facto,* the very sort of person who *needs* to keep one. Remember our story in Chapter One about the tree cutter who didn't think he had time to stop and sharpen his saw? Contrary to what you might think, it doesn't take long. If you keep your time log close at hand, and write down things *while they're happening,* you'll find that it takes almost no time at all because much of your recording is done while the activity is taking place. You'll also be ensuring that you won't forget things.

A third frequent comment about time logs is this pained protest from people after completing their first one: "I know it looks bad, but I can explain this. Today wasn't a normal day. I usually don't have so much going wrong!" In all my years of teaching people about time management, I have yet to see a "normal" day. One salesperson, stunned to discover that he spent only 19 percent of his time on his number-one priority, said, "If I wait for a normal day, I'll be dead."

A detailed time inventory is necessary, because the painful task of changing our habits requires more conviction than we can build from learning about the experience of others. We need the incentive that comes from seeing the amazing revelations of the great portions of time we ourselves are wasting. There is simply no other way to get the information we need.

How to Keep a Time Log

For at least three days, maintain a scrupulously detailed accounting of all your activities. A week is probably better, especially if your job is cyclical and certain things come up only on certain days of the week. These are the specific steps:

1. Note today's date; list three to six key goals for the day, tasks you *must* accomplish. (Refer back to Chapter Three for discussion of goals and priorities, if needed.) Set a deadline for each one.

2. Record each activity as the day progresses. Every time your attention shifts from one thing to another, write down the diverting activity, no matter how trivial. This means that you will record all interruptions, noting their sources and their reasons. Give as much detail as possible

3. Make a note of how much time you spent on each item.

4. Set a priority for every single item. The point is that at the end of the day you will look back and see what proportion of time was spent on high-priority work. Use this weighting:

> 1 = Important and urgent (must)
> 2 = Important (should)
> 3 = Routine (could do, or delegate)
> 4 = Wasted (why did I do that?)

5. In a "Comments" column, record your ideas on how you might have done things better. Some people like to go back and do this at the end of the day, thinking the passage of time gives them a somewhat better perspective. I recommend that you write your comments as you go along; this minimizes the possibility of forgetting the details.

Paper or Computer?

Traditionally time logs have been kept by hand, on a form like the one used by Elizabeth in Figure 2. I suggest keeping it close at hand so you can enter activities while you are doing them.

Figure 2. Elizabeth's time log.

Date _Sept. 15_

Goals for Today

Rank	Goal	Deadline	Rank	Goal	Deadline
1	write contract	10:30	4	corresp.	4:00
2	report to S.K.	11:00			
3	agenda-staff mtg.	12:00			

Priorities for Evaluating Logged Activities:

1 = Important and Urgent (Must)   3 = Routine (Could or Delegate)
2 = Important (Should)   4 = Wasted (Why did I do that?)

Time	Activity	Time Used	Priority	Comments
8:05	Read newspaper	25	4	Read during lunch
8:30	check phone messages	5	2	Mary could prioritize for me
8:36	Return C→BR (re Mill)	5	2	good time for phone— she's in but not yet swamped
8:41	→ C-Sh (picnic)	5	4	not inept problem
8:46	X Mary? ltr. (Jones)	2	3	early a.m. review would take care of
8:48	coffee, talk w. Bill M. (Chas.)	10	4	gossip is fun but...
8:58	open, read mail	25	4	Mary could open & sort
				and handle some—me do reading late p.m.
9:23	dictate draft contract	7	1	need info from WH
9:27	C→ WH for contr. info	3	1	he's not avail—left msg
9:30	resume dictation	14	1	dictating equip. would
				Save 2 people's time
9:44	X→C SK re report	4	2	oops! way behind
				sched. Have until
				11:00 to meet deadline

When you answer the phone, write down the phone call; when you're talking with a drop-in visitor, unobtrusively reach over and jot it down on the log sheet; when you start to sign letters, sign in on the log first.

Use abbreviations and shortcuts. Denote people and projects by their initials. Indicate interruptions with a big X. A question mark by someone's initials can be your shorthand for "had a question." For phone calls, use a capital C, with an arrow pointing to the C for calls that come in and an arrow pointing away from it for calls you make.

$$\to C = \text{incoming call} \qquad C \to = \text{outgoing call}$$

You can also maintain your log on your computer. Use your favorite spreadsheet software or follow the format of the sample log in Figure 2 and set up your columns accordingly. Your program may be able to insert the time automatically whenever you make an entry and maintain a running total of the time invested. Create macros or devise supershortcuts for frequently used names and words. At the end of the day you will quickly be able to sort types and categories of activities, and get an instant total of the minutes spent in each one. Then, at the end of the week, you can obtain the data that will show patterns of activities and results.

Cautions for Your Time Log

If you've never done a time log before, brush up on these points before you start each day:

1. Every single time you shift your attention, record the new item. Don't make the common mistake of noting what you're doing at fixed intervals, say every fifteen minutes; you simply miss too much that way.

2. Be very specific. The value of the log is severely watered down if you use very general language. If you note a ten-minute block as merely "phone calls," you won't be able to tell at the end of the day which were necessary and which were time-wasting interruptions. You won't even be able to judge whether the

time spent on the necessary calls was warranted or partially wasted.

3. Record *everything*. Don't skip over daydreaming, socializing, brief interruptions just because they seem minor at the time. You're trying to determine how much of your *total* time is frittered *away* in such "minor" activities.

4. Log your time *as you go*.

5. Do it all day long; don't try to catch up at the end of the day. This is probably the most serious mistake of all. You simply won't remember, even if you think you will—no one's memory is that good. Then too, if you're doing it all at once, the temptation to make yourself look good will be nearly irresistible. If you're recording throughout the day, this tendency is less likely to be a problem.

6. Be totally honest if you want to gain the most from this experience. After all, no one needs to see the time log but you. So don't fool yourself.

Free Side Benefit

The greatest benefit of a time log is that it helps you identify your real problems relating to time use. It forces you to face reality so that you can take corrective action in a meaningful way.

But there is a terrific side benefit, and it's free; it takes no additional effort on your part. The discipline of writing things down creates an automatic self-correction. Because writing it down forces us to be aware of what we are doing, we tend to catch our mistakes while they are happening, and correct ourselves on the spot. What's more, this self-correction is virtually automatic; it requires almost no conscious effort.

Analyzing Your Time Log

The next step is to take a good hard look at your log and discover what it has to tell you. Be honest with yourself; if you aren't, your efforts at keeping the log will be wasted. Ask your-self these questions:

1. What time did you start on your number-one goal?
   a. Could you have started sooner?
   b. Did anything distract you from completing it?
   c. Could you have avoided the distraction?
   d. Once distracted, did you recover immediately and re-turn to the task at once?
2. What was your longest period of totally uninterrupted time? (Don't count lunch or meetings.)
3. What was your most productive period? Least productive?
4. To what extent did you achieve your main goals for the day?

	Goal	Percent Accomplished
a.	_____	_____
b.	_____	_____
c.	_____	_____
d.	_____	_____
e.	_____	_____

5. Were you following a written plan based on the day's priori-ties?
6. Were you doing the right job at the right time?
7. What did you do that you should not have been doing? Could it have been delegated?
8. How could you have done what you were doing more ef-fectively? More simply? In less detail?
9. Concerning interruptions:
   a. Were the interruptions for items more important than the interrupted task?
   b. Count the interruptions in each category to find the worst offenders: Telephone? Visitors? Crises? Self? Assis-

tant? Team member? Clients? Meetings too long? Unnecessary meetings?
   c. Are you needlessly interrupting others?
10. Concerning your contact/communications with others:
   a. Are they important enough to be worth it?
   b. Do they take too long?
   c. Are you dealing with the right person each time?
   d. Were your contacts inefficient because you lacked notes of earlier discussions and follow-up items?
11. How much time was spent on paperwork? Can that be curtailed by being more organized? Is a poor filing system costing you time looking for information?
12. Do you have an effective system for monitoring progress on projects—yours and those you delegated?
13. Was time waiting or traveling spent productively? How could it have been?
14. Did jobs have to be redone because of haste or impatience?
15. Was your time spent in proportion to your priorities?

Considering these questions, it doesn't take long to spot Elizabeth's mistakes:

- In the first hour and a half, only one top-priority item was addressed. This violates the time management axiom: *Get number one done first!*
- The number-one job might have been completed in the first twenty minutes of the day if the necessary information had been requested at the right time.
- The interruptions on the contract job meant delays and still no resolution.

The Case of the Candid Sales Manager

Now let's analyze a tougher case. Bill R., a sales manager for the food group of a large consumer products corporation, kept the time log you see in Figure 3. First we'll see what Bill himself says about his time use, then we'll examine his analysis. Fortunately for us—and for him—Bill is a pretty candid guy.

Figure 3. Bill's time log.

Date _March 12_

Goals for Today

Rank	Goal	Deadline	Rank	Goal	Deadline
1	Finish mgt. review	10:00	4	Staff meeting	11:00
2	Sales summary to boss	1:00	5	catch up on mail	4:00
3	Service report to boss	2:00	6	resolve Brown problem	5:00

Priorities for Evaluating Logged Activities:

1 = Important and Urgent (must)   3 = Routine (Could or Delegate)
2 = Important (Should)   4 = Wasted (Why did I do that?)

Time	Activity	Time Used	Priority	Comments
8:10	get coffee : read W.S. journal	20	4	can read at lunch; first 20 min. wasted
8:30	review plan for today	15	1	well spent; found 2 problems to alert Helen to
8:45	misc notes to Helen	5	1	good use of time
8:50	wife called	15	4	Sw'board could have taken msg.
9:05	BB called re budget	15	3	ditto
9:20	dictation, Helen	45	2	not really organized for this dictation
10:05	read and separated mail	30	4	Helen can do; have her sort + prioritize + answer some
10:35	boss came by; chat re trip (personal)	16	4	act busy; be candid when boss drops in
10:51	coffee	9	4	not necy — habit
11:00	Staff mtg. ↓ Space allocation discussion	60	2??	could have been done in 30 min — don't even get in to space issue — not an issue for entire staff.
12:00	sign mail	20	4	Helen could sign routine mail
12:20	lunch ↓	65	4	could have met w. boss at lunch + completed sales sum. but not ready when he suggested it
1:25	complete sales summary for 2:00 mtg.	5	1	urgent now because left till last minute
1:30	CS dropped in - social	12	4	unnec. interrup'n
1:42	BB called re budget	13	4	ditto

Time	Activity	Time Used	Priority	Comments
1:55	called JD re personnel	5	4	ditto; this could wait
2:00	mtg w boss-sales sum.	45	2	if written report had been submitted earlier, boss could have reviewed; then this meeting could be cut
	↓			
[2:30	boss oks delay on			to 15 min or even elim. If he had returned it to me
	service report]			w. questions – 30 min wasted.
2:45	Rm call, info systems in to ask boss when to expect decision re dept reorganization	17	2	no one else could handle
3:02	JJ called - personnel item	5	4	Refer to HC
3:07	Rm dropped in, Qu on info for new system	8	4	Refer to Hank
3:15	go for coffee	15	4	don't need it!
3:30	distrib. mtg	60	4	attended out of habit; so some qu. to me that Hank could handle. From now on leave these mtgs to Hank unless he asks me to sit in.
	↓			
4:30	worked on mgt review	3	1	this was #1 for day but left until end and then
4:33	interruption by Tm re staff mtg	7	4	permitted interruption could easily wait till next mtg.
4:40	back to mgt. review	15	1	not much accomplished
4:55	call pers. re Brown– too late	5	2	procras. Killed this one
5:10	home			where did day go???

Let's see what he says about setting and abiding by daily goals:
"What time did you start your number-one goal?"
   4:30.
"Could you have started sooner?"
   Yes.
"Did anything distract you from completing it?"
   Yes, interrupted by TM, but late start real cause.
"Did you recover immediately after the distraction?"
   No. Too late. (He probably means too late in the day to get started.)

So we learn that Bill is not inclined to pull his punches. He is honest with himself, and that's an excellent start. Now, the questions about periods of productivity:

"What was your longest period of uninterrupted work time alone?"
   Thirty minutes.
"What was your most productive period?"
   Early in the morning and late afternoon.

Bill's answers are typical; many people would say those are their most productive times. But Bill is fooling himself. The very first thing he did was get coffee and read *The Wall Street Journal*. Neither is a top-priority task; Bill may be correct in his assessment that early morning is when he is freshest and most alert, but he certainly did not use that period productively. In the late afternoon, when he finally got to his number-one job, he may have felt mentally ready to tackle the task, but he was *not* productive, for he permitted what he himself calls a needless interruption.

"What was your least productive period?"
   9:30 to 10:30 and 2:45 to 3:30.

Notice Bill doesn't say anything about the time spent in meetings, yet a look at his log shows that those were not productive activities. The staff meeting apparently wasted a half hour; the forty-five-minute meeting with the boss might have been handled another way; and the distributor meeting, another hour, might have been handled by one of his team. So that's more than two hours unwisely spent, almost totally wasted, in meetings. Add to that the one and three quarters hours that Bill tags "least productive," and you see that four hours—half a work day— were poorly spent.

"To what extent did you achieve your main goals?"

Bill is honest about the incomplete results, but rationalizes the causes. Let's examine this part of the analysis in some detail, for it teaches us a great deal:

Goal	Percent Completed	Bill's Reason for Noncompletion
#1	20%	"Late start, interrupted; too little time"
#2	100	"Had to get it done (boss)"
#3	0	"Boss OK'd delay"
#4	100	"Routine"
#5	0	"Only able to stay even; too much to do"
#6	0	"Other things more important"

Understandably, Bill's explanation of his reasons are some- what defensive. But if he is serious about time management, he must see his "reasons" for the excuses they are. "Late start" and "interruptions" are nothing more than rationalizations, for Bill *permitted* these to interfere with his number-one goal. The excuse of "too little time" is meaningless; like everyone else, Bill has all the time there is.

The boss provided the motivation for completing the sec- ond goal of the day—and the excuse for *not* completing the third. Then we come to the staff meeting. It was 100 percent completed, but what does that mean, really? Bill phrased this goal as an activity—"hold a staff meeting"—instead of concen- trating on the results to be achieved in the meeting. A better goal might have been to *avoid* holding a staff meeting, especially as Bill appears to consider half of the hour a waste. A staff meeting is a routine item; it has no place on a serious list of daily goals.

Similarly, it is difficult to believe that Bill's goal of "catching up on mail" would forward a long-range objective. Furthermore, Bill handled this routine task ineffectively. At 10:05 he apparently spent thirty minutes separating mail—that's a job for his assistant. But when he sat down to "catch up," he could manage only to stay even, because there was "too much to do."

The Brown matter did not get resolved because "other things [were] more important." But what were these other things? Where do they appear on the time log? If they were indeed more important, they would show up in the list of daily goals, in the sequence of their true significance.

Now we come to the question of interruptions. In this area Bill is woefully unaware of the real psychological forces at work. He's in good company—so is most of the rest of the world.

"What type of interruptions usually occur in your job, and how could you control them?"

Bill's answers here are very revealing:

1. Unexpected crises   *No real solution; hazard of the business.*
2. Unscheduled meetings   *When the boss calls them, you go.*
3. Phone interruptions   *Have secretary screen.*
4. Drop-in visitors   *We have an open-door policy.*

In three out of the four biggest time concerns, Bill concluded there was nothing he could do. He's wrong. There are solid, workable ways to avoid or limit every one of these common problems, as you will see in Part Two. But we don't expect Bill to know that yet; for now we are pleased that the time log has done its job: pointed out the problems.

"Who interrupted you the most?"
   Boss and associates and team. But all necessary!

Bill has right in front of him the evidence that points to the *true* source of interruptions—himself; he just doesn't see it. At approximately 8:10 he read the *Journal,* later noting that he could have read it over lunch. This is a *self*-interruption. At 8:50 he was interrupted by two phone calls, but noted that the switchboard operator could have taken messages. At 9:30 he gets fouled up in dictation by not being prepared, thus dictating matters the assistant should have handled, which is another form of self-interruption. Then he separated mail instead of delegating that routine matter to his secretary. Next his boss interrupted on a personal matter, and Bill admits he should have been candid about being busy. And so on throughout the day. Self-interruption is usually the biggest time-wasting culprit of all.

"What were the causes of the interruptions?"
Emergencies and other necessary communications.

I don't see a single emergency on Bill's log, and few "necessary" communications. In fact, looking over what Bill considers "necessary" interruptions, I would guess there are many other smaller ones that did not get noted on the log. Numerous studies show that the average manager is interrupted once every eight minutes during a typical day.

"How could you eliminate interruptions?"
They are my job, so why would I eliminate them?

This is an example of our old friend, human nature, at work. We want to think that interruptions are legitimate, that they are significant enough to warrant putting aside whatever we are doing. Otherwise why would we allow this to happen to us? In answering this question, Bill is obviously thinking of *serious* interruptions, which would indeed be part of his job. His mistake, a very common one, is that he has failed to recognize reality: Most of his interruptions that day were minor, even trivial.

The Next Step

Each in his or her own way, Bill and Elizabeth have demonstrated the process of keeping a time log, and analyzing the patterns it reveals. This is their first step in planning how to solve their time problems—and it is also yours. Keep a time log for several days, three at least, and analyze what it tells you about your current time management habit. Then you will be ready to turn to Part Two, and begin the "remodeling" process.

Part Two

The Twenty Biggest Time Wasters and How to Cure Them

1. Management by Crisis
2. Telephone Interruptions
3. Inadequate Planning
4. Attempting Too Much
5. Drop-in Visitors
6. Ineffective Delegation
7. Personal Disorganization
8. Lack of Self-Discipline
9. Inability to Say No
10. Procrastination
11. Meetings
12. Paperwork
13. Leaving Tasks Unfinished
14. Inadequate Staff
15. Socializing
16. Confused Responsibility or Authority
17. Poor Communication
18. Inadequate Controls and Progress Reports
19. Incomplete Information
20. Travel

Management by Crisis

1

"If anything can go wrong, it will." Murphy's famous law has become so well known that it now appears on wall plaques, coffee mugs, and bumper stickers. There is a tendency to view it as nothing more than a clever saying, maybe even a joke. But infamy makes the idea no less true. Things *do* have a way of going wrong . . . and usually will, unless we take measures to prevent it.

Crisis management has corporate America by the throat. Experienced managers tell me that when they think they've seen every possible sort of crisis a new one pops up. The crisis may come from around any corner, may involve any person at any level in the organization, and may take just about any shape, but the consequences are dismayingly similar.

A crisis will divert you from your own priorities for the day. An important deadline rushes toward you, but you're stuck with resolving the crisis. The information you need from someone else is late—or insufficient. Your boss compounds the pressure by adding on other assignments. In the middle of the job, something else goes wrong. Tension mounts; tempers flare. Blame gets directed outward, and the circle of damage gets wider and wider. Of all the time concerns, nothing has a more devastating impact on morale than crisis management. Its ultimate cost, if we could measure it, would surely exceed anything we could imagine.

Is It Really a Crisis?

How many times have you heard someone say—or said yourself—"I didn't get anything important accomplished because I spent all day putting out fires"? Firefighting is not crisis handling. A firefighter is someone who doesn't know how to anticipate, cannot keep the big picture in mind, but lives from moment to moment. Firefighters continually have problems erupting around them, and they race around madly trying to quiet them. Their days are a frantic jumble of small emergencies that never should have happened.

A genuine crisis, on the other hand, can be defined as an unexpected interruption from the normal course of events that is of such major importance that it necessitates immediate response. *Major* importance requiring *immediate* response. For example:

- The messenger service loses the package containing original artwork for the animation sequence—three months' work.
- A fire destroys all the accounting records.
- The agency's major client, which generates more than half the annual billings, announces it is switching to another agency.
- A key person resigns in the middle of a big project.

Winston Churchill gave us a lesson in proportion. That wise man took a nap every day in his later years, leaving instructions that he was to be awakened only in the event of a crisis. "And," he said, "I further define a crisis to be the armed invasion of the British Isles."

Planning Prevents Crises

Management by crisis means dealing with a crisis *after* it occurs. But the best way to handle a crisis is to keep it from occurring in the first place. And the best way to do that is to anticipate what might happen and make plans to prevent it, if possible, or if not, to reduce its impact. That, in a nutshell, is the solution to this number-one time waster.

But, you say, how can I know what will go wrong? It's impossible to predict what will happen next around here. If I *knew* what was going to happen, I could plan for it. But a crisis is unpredictable—that's what makes it a crisis.

My response to that is to ask you whether you have the police emergency number posted somewhere near your phone at home, or a first-aid kit in your camping gear. Of course you do. You don't know *when* you may need them, but you know there's a reasonably good chance that you will at some point, and so you have taken commonsense precautions.

In a work setting the process is essentially the same. You cannot predict *when* a crisis will occur, but with careful planning you can at least alleviate it when it *does* occur. You may even be able to prevent it. Get in the habit of always asking yourself, "What could go wrong here?" Then, "What else could go wrong? And what else?" The more critical the undertaking is, the more important it is to try to anticipate the trouble spots.

Contingency Planning

The technique of anticipating problems and preventing them, or minimizing their consequences, is called contingency planning. It is your most powerful crisis-control tool.

In its simplest form, contingency planning involves these three steps:

1. Identify potential problems. Use what you have learned from past projects, other people's experiences, common sense. Think of all the steps involved in the project, and for each one, keep asking yourself, "What could go wrong?"
2. Rank them in priority order, considering both degree of seriousness and probability of occurrence.

3. Develop steps to prevent them or to limit their consequences.

The process is illustrated by the sample contingency matrix shown in Figure 4. After you have listed potential problems, consider how likely each one is, and how serious it would be if it did happen. Use a three-point scale, with 1 for the most serious or most likely. Then add the assigned points for each problem to derive a weighted priority. The one with the lowest number is your most serious concern.

Now, think through the steps that will prevent or defuse each crisis. In the example here, the biggest problem is the possible loss of a key person, and so this is where you put your attention first. You have realized that your project manager is showing signs of restlessness, and it seems likely that she might resign. As the supervisor, you would talk with her to identify the problem and work toward solving it. That way, you may be able to prevent the crisis from happening. At the same time, you will cover your bases by training other team members in the critical skills so that if this key person does leave, others can step in and take over some of the project responsibilities.

Then, once you have outlined preventive steps for the first problem, do the same for the second, and so on down your list.

Lessons From the Past

One important source of information for contingency planning is your own past history. In similar situations in the past, what happened? Where did trouble suddenly show up? In every crisis experience you should always look for lessons. When it's all over, assign your team to do a postmortem; record what went wrong and analyze what can be done to prevent it in the future.

This is one positive benefit that can come from crises, and yet very few managers make the effort. Perhaps the demands of solving the problem have taken all their energy, and they mentally collapse when it is over. This is an aspect of human nature that you should make an effort to overcome. Don't let valuable information slip away.

Figure 4. Sample contingency matrix.

I. Potential Problems	II. Priority Analysis			III. Steps to	
	A. How Serious	B. How Probable	C. Weighted Priority	A. Prevent	B. Limit
1. Strike	2	2	4		
2. Key person loss	1	1	(2)	communicate to ensure satisfaction	cross train
3. Fire, Flood, etc.	3	3	6		
4. Major sale revoked	2	3	5		
5. Major failure of product or service	1	2	3		

1 = Most serious or likely.
3 = Least serious or likely

Adapted from Charles Kepner and Benjamin Tregoe, *The Rational Manager* (New York: McGraw-Hill, 1965), pp. 224–226.

Give Yourself a Cushion

One sure way to prevent a crisis is to give yourself time to catch a minor problem before it escalates into something major. Recognize that everything takes longer than you think it will (another one of Murphy's laws), so build in a cushion. Set a deadline and then move it forward by at least 20 percent. Structure projects to include regular progress reports so you will know in time to make changes should anything slip off track. (More on this in Time Topic 18.) Also, if you know you are vulnerable to procrastination (see Time Topic 10), be aware of the negative connection to crisis development, and be extra vigilant.

Overreaction—The Hero Syndrome

Time spent solving crises that never should have occurred is time wasted. Time spent solving problems that never should have occurred and are not really of crisis proportion is wasted even more foolishly.

Many managers, especially in crisis-prone organizations, tend to overreact when problems are brought to them. Partly they are suffering from the hero syndrome: letting things build to a crisis level, or making a crisis out of what started as a manageable problem, so that they can demonstrate what a hero they are. Once again, human nature enters the picture. It is very understandable, but also very damaging.

Always ask yourself, "Do I really need to get involved here? What's the worst that would happen if I did nothing?" Panic is contagious. Doing nothing is far better than "managing" the situation into a crisis. If the problem can be ignored, ignore it. If you can't ignore it, delegate it to one of your team. You yourself should step in only if no one else can handle things.

In short, don't overreact, and don't allow your team to do it. When someone rushes in and blurts, "We've got a *big* problem here," don't let his sense of urgency infect you. If it turns out the situation is not really a crisis after all, say something like this:

"Wait a second, Harry. This is starting to sound different. At first I thought we had a real crisis, but now it seems more like the kind of problem that's right up your alley. Actually, it's the sort of problem I for one am glad we have, or we wouldn't need good people like you around. Why don't you take this back and go over it a bit. Figure out what you think ought to be done, then come back and give me two or three alternatives and let me know your recommendation. Okay?"

Don't Shoot the Messenger

One very interesting source that contributes to the development of a crisis is the reluctance of team members to tell the boss when things go wrong. If they delay imparting bad news because they fear the boss's reaction, they use up the time that could be applied to correcting the situation.

The solution here is to foster a climate in which mistakes are accepted. Let your people know that you consider mistakes part of the learning process. Emphasize in a nonthreatening way that fast reporting of bad news will enable you to catch a problem at a stage when it can easily be repaired.

And if you are the person who must deliver the bad news, but you're uneasy about what the reaction will be, make your presentation along these lines:

"If I were you, I'd be hoping for a good report about now. Unfortunately, that's just not possible at the moment. We all believe, and we have good reasons, that the situation will improve very soon. But I thought it would be a mistake not to let you know the disappointing news now, because you may have some ideas. So, if you'd prefer to wait for the good news that we're pretty sure will be coming soon, I'll come back later. If you'd like the not-so-good news now, I'm ready. Which will it be?"

Check Yourself

Do you manage by crises or prevent them? Rank yourself on the following; then do it again three months from now.

Almost never = 0
Sometimes = 1
Half the time = 2
Usually = 3
Almost always = 4

Points

1. I anticipate things that can go wrong and take action to prevent them or to limit their consequences. _____
2. I require regular progress reports on all major tasks so I can identify problems in time to take corrective action. _____
3. Whenever goals and objectives have been set, I examine all reasonable alternatives for achieving them so I can determine which is least likely to generate crises. _____
4. When managing crisis situations, I avoid overcommitment of resources by determining who and what are really needed to handle the situation. _____
5. After a crisis, I ask those involved what happened and what steps can be taken to avoid a repetition. Then I implement suitable steps immediately. _____
6. I build cushions into my day to allow time to respond to unforeseen crises. _____

Total _____

Telephone Interruptions

There is something wholly irresistible about a ringing telephone. The imperious tone of the ring demands, "Pick me up. I may have important news for you." In a work setting, probably not one person in a thousand can sit by a phone that is ringing and ignore it. Yet tune it out you must, for telephone interruptions can shatter your concentration and fracture your productivity as nothing else can.

The irony is that this time waster is one of the easiest to cure. Once it is recognized, that is. Many people simply don't believe they spend as much time on the phone as they do, or they tend to say things like "But I *have* to take these calls. It might be _____ [*fill in the blank:* my boss, our big client, someone who needs to talk to me]."

Those who don't think they spend much time on phone calls should keep a time log; it can show with stark clarity just how much time telephone interruptions eat up. If you have doubts, do a targeted time log on this one problem (see Part Three). Remember, the problem is not just the time that the interruption itself consumes, but the time you need to catch up mentally to where you were before you were interrupted.

To those who insist they *have* to take their calls, I would ask, "But do you have to take them *now*, at this moment? And when you do, do you really have to talk so long?" For there are two aspects to the telephone problem: the interruption factor, and the efficiency factor. You will learn how to deal with both here.

Human Nature

A lot of our problems with the telephone involve questions of human nature. That strong tug that says "Answer me" comes not from the phone but from our own psyche. Here are some of the reasons the telephone has such a hold on us:

- Presumption of legitimacy. We *assume* that every call is a legitimate demand for our attention, and if we interrupt our own work to answer the call, we are by default concluding that whatever the caller wants is *more* important than whatever we are doing at the time.
- Fear of offending. We answer phone calls when we shouldn't, and talk longer than we should, because we fear causing offense to the callers if we do otherwise.
- Desire to keep informed, not to be left out of anything that may be happening. You see this in action when people subconsciously pause and listen while their assistant answers the phone. The urge to know who it is and what it's about is strong indeed.
- Ego. The fact that others call *us* for the information makes us feel important.
- Pleasure of socializing. Some people cannot resist turning every call into a social occasion; the business part must wait until after the visiting.
- A handy excuse. If we are reluctant to take up a difficult (or boring) task, answering "important" phone calls provides a wonderful rationale for procrastinating.

Human nature, as we know, is a powerful force indeed. The trick is to recognize it, accept it, and not let it cripple you. Take what you have learned about integrating new habits, and begin developing a new way of thinking about the telephone. It is not a humanoid with a life of its own. It is a tool for communication—no less, but definitely no more.

Blocking Interruptions

The number-one underlying cause of telephone interruptions is your presumption of legitimacy. And so the number-one solution is to ditch the idea that the caller's need is necessarily more important than your need to concentrate on your work.

Screening

The macro solution to telephone interruptions is to screen your calls so that you do not have to stop each time the phone rings. You can then return the call at a time that is convenient for *you*.

Start by discussing your intention with your assistant if you have one. Decide which categories of calls you want to accept right away; for instance, family emergencies, your boss, company VIPs, major clients. Or perhaps you want your assistant to hold all calls except emergencies. Work out a definition of what constitutes an "emergency." For all others, your assistant will take messages for callbacks, including a brief notation of what the call is about so that you can be fully prepared and efficient when you return the call. Then, using your ideal day (see Chapter Three in Part One), assign regular time blocks for returning phone calls. Many people like to do this right after lunch and again toward the end of the day.

The four basic steps in the screening hierarchy are:

1. *Handle.* Whenever possible, the assistant answers the caller's questions, arranges for the material, takes down the information about the meeting, and so on.
2. *Refer.* If the assistant is unable to handle the call, she will next try to refer the caller to someone else in the organization who is in a position to help.
3. *Postpone.* If the situation is something only you can handle, the assistant will try to avoid interrupting you by taking a message so that you can return the call at a later time.
4. *Expedite.* If it falls within predetermined guidelines

(emergency or VIP), the assistant will put the call through.

Tips for Tactful Screening

All of us have felt the frustration and insult of not being allowed to speak to the person we called. No doubt it is the memory of these unfortunate experiences that makes some people reluctant to have their own calls screened; they don't want to risk offending a client, an important supplier, or anyone else. This concern is understandable, but groundless. A skilled assistant can deflect interruptions without offending the caller in any way. If you sense that some coaching might be helpful in this area, try some of the following suggestions.

With most callers, a polite businesslike approach is sufficient: "I'm sorry, she's not available at the moment. May she call you back when she's free?" The caller has little choice but to concur, and so the assistant takes down the name, phone number, and the caller's organization, if necessary, and then asks the purpose of the call: "May I add a brief note of what this is about so she can be prepared when she calls back?"

The answer to this last question is the key, and a savvy caller will say something like this: "I'm preparing the budget draft for the committee meeting tomorrow, and I need to get her opinion on something before I can finish up. Tell her I probably need only about five minutes, but it does have to be sometime today."

Once she has determined the purpose of the call, the astute assistant knows what to do next:

- *Handle:* "I think I know the report you mean; would you like to hold while I look in our files?"
- *Refer:* "Actually, our head designer is working on that project this afternoon; would you like me to transfer you over to him?"
- *Postpone:* "I believe she'll be able to call you back around 11:00; would that be all right?"
- *Expedite:* "I'll see if I can interrupt her."

Your assistant's effectiveness in all this depends on your wholehearted support. She is doing her job; *your* job is to back her up. If someone is irritated by the screening process, you must support your assistant 100 percent, unless it is clear she has made a serious transgression. Don't let callers trample on her.

Not long ago I watched an outstanding young manager defend his assistant brilliantly. The caller came on the line and gruffly demanded, "Who on earth do you have working for you these days? Do you know what she did? When I asked for you she demanded 'What's it about?' and in just that tone of voice."

"Well," the manager calmly replied, "if she did speak that way, it's the first time in the five years that she has performed for me as the best executive assistant I've ever had. I will talk to her later, and ask for her side of the story, but in the meantime, what can I do for you?" Without actually calling the person a liar, he very effectively squelched this officious complaint.

If You Don't Have an Assistant

If you do not have someone to screen your calls, there are many other ways to control the phone. Here are a few ideas:

- The first and most obvious way is to use an answering machine. A wide range of possibilities from a simple recorded message to the most sophisticated voice mail system permits you to choose the features that truly meet your needs. As with any tool or electronic device from the telephone to the most complex computer organizer, what counts in achieving results are the consistency and discipline with which you *use* the tool to achieve your goals and priorities. As of this writing, no electronic devices have lives of their own, unless we permit them to do so.
- Work out a deal with colleagues. You cover their phone for a while, then they'll cover yours.
- Some people use mechanical aids like a cut-off switch or a blinking light to replace the ringing mechanism. With a cut-off switch, you can temporarily block calls. And you

can train yourself to ignore the light (or move the phone out of your line of sight).

- Take your work and go somewhere in the building where there are no phones.

E-mail can be more efficient than phoning, especially for someone who is hard to reach. Both senders and receivers can communicate accurate, specific messages in written form at their own convenience. The disadvantage can be a glut of e-mail you feel compelled to answer. Then—just as in keeping up with computer technology—what started out as an electronic *time-saver* can become an electronic *time waster*.

You and Your Boss

Another kind of telephone interruption, one that happens all too often, occurs in the boss's office: You are working with her on something and she continues to interrupt your meeting to take calls from others. If this jeopardizes your own time, or if it is becoming a serious problem, here's what to do.

Take a piece of paper and write on it: "I can see you're busy. I'll go back to my desk and continue on the XYZ Project I'm working on for you. Give me a buzz when you're free." Then fold it two or three times, place it on her desk, and leave. Don't slide the unfolded paper toward her; she may just nonverbally signal you to sit back down and wait. If the note is folded several times, by the time she gets it unfolded, especially with just one hand, you're gone.

A smart manager is going to realize that you've done the right thing. When you get together again, you may even say something like this: "Say, do you think you could have Ellen hold your calls for just a bit? I think we can finish this up in about five minutes."

The Quiet Hour

The quiet hour takes screening to a higher level. For a certain period of time—maybe an hour, maybe more—everyone in the organization has the luxury of uninterrupted concentration. By mutual agreement, no one in the company calls, and no one drops in to visit.

Details on the quiet hour are explained in Time Topic 3. The question here is what to do about telephone calls that come in from outside the company during this period. If the quiet hour is to be effective, your assistant should make every effort to keep all but the most important calls from you, even those that at other times of the day she might decide to put through: "I'm sorry, but she's not available at the moment. I can have her call you back at 10:00, if you like."

Even with some important clients you may wish to reinforce the plan by saying something like this; "I have asked my assistant to screen calls and visitors between 9:00 and 10:00, and I use that time for strategic planning on your account as well as those of others. However, I've told her to put you through if you call during that hour." The chances are very good that your client will go out of his way *not* to call then.

Handling Calls Efficiently

Let's say you've done everything right. You've had your assistant screen your calls, you have a stack of messages for callbacks, and it's the scheduled time for returning calls. First, get organized. Collect all the files and other backup information you need; check your notes from your last conversation with the callers. Then have some routine work you can do while on the phone— signing mail, for instance.

Many people prefer to place their own calls, but I recommend that you have your assistant do this for you, if possible. It can be a real time saver because usually less than one in three calls goes through and those that do are apt to reach an involved phone menu. Don't play telephone tag. If the person you're calling is not in, find out when he or she will be available, and don't call at any other time. Make an appointment to call at a specific time. Don't leave an "empty" message; leave word what you're calling about so both of you can proceed smoothly when you do connect. If the person is busy when you call, don't allow your-

> *Batch your calls.*
> *Return them all in a block.*
> *Work on something else at*
> *the same time.*

self to be put on hold—unless it's someone who is extraordinarily difficult to reach; in that case it may be faster in the long run to wait.

Placing your own calls can save time if—as in e-mail—you and the other party are very good at leaving succinct, to-the-point messages. But always make sure you have work you can do effectively while you are on hold. Many people use either speaker phones or handset attachments or simply cradle the phone under their ear to enable them to continue to work at their computers while they are on hold.

Good Phone Techniques

Over the years I have talked with many businesspeople about the problem of the telephone. The average phone call takes six minutes, yet most people say they could have concluded their calls in two minutes if they had been more efficient.

Set a time limit for each call. A three-minute egg timer may look silly on your desk, but it serves the purpose very nicely. After a while, you may decide it isn't so silly after all.

The most critical point in a call is the first sentence; this is what sets the tone: businesslike and professional, or social chitchat. We all have a strong inclination to answer the question that is asked us; you can use this tendency to good advantage in business phone calls.

If you're placing the call, start out on a business footing:

Don't say: "Hello, Louise. How's the weather out there in Seattle?"

Instead say: "Hello, Louise; this is Jeff. I know you're busy too; I just have one quick question about the Bermuda contract, okay?"

This way, even if Louise is in the mood to socialize, she will focus on the contract instead, because that's what you asked her about. If you do ask about the weather, or her family, she will of course answer and then feel obliged to ask about *your* family or *your* weather, and both of you have wasted time.

Similarly, if you're receiving the call, give your very first sentence a business orientation:

Don't say: "Hi there, Chuck. How was the vacation?"

Instead say: "Hi there, Chuck. What can I do for you?"

Here's a technique for long-winded callers. Interrupt them in mid-sentence and say, "Oh, Pete, excuse me just one moment. Looks like we have a minor emergency here. Do you want me to call you back, or would you rather hold?" If Pete is really a talker, he'll probably hold, so go do some quick task and then come back on the line and say, "Sorry about that, Pete. I'm going to have to go in a minute. Real quick now, what can I do for you?" One caution: Know whom you're dealing with; don't try this in a first-time encounter.

Many people seem to lack the ability to terminate a conversation smoothly and efficiently. Try these approaches:

- *Cue the ending.* "Kim, before we hang up, I want to be sure we're clear about this one point."
- *Mention your time limit.* "I just have a minute before I have to leave for a meeting; was there anything else you need?"
- *Be candid.* "Joe, I'm gonna have to leave it here; the boss is expecting something from me in a few minutes. See you Saturday."

Check Yourself

How successful are you at managing telephone interruptions? Rank yourself on the following; then do it again three months from now.

Almost never   = 0
Sometimes   = 1
Half the time   = 2
Usually   = 3
Almost always   = 4

Points

1. My phone calls are screened effectively.   _____
2. I time-limit my telephone calls by a monitoring device on my phone, a three-minute egg timer, or a reminder from my assistant.   _____
3. Before accepting a phone call, I ask its purpose in order to determine its relative priority.   _____
4. Before proceeding with a call, I explore alternative solutions, such as what efforts, if any, the interrupter has made to solve the problem; who else might be equally or better situated to help; whether postponing action might be in everyone's best interests; and what the consequences of no action might be.
5. I use a mechanical answering device, voice mail, or a cut-off switch whenever appropriate.   _____

                                                      Total   _____

Inadequate Planning

Remember Paul Barrington (Chapter Three), who came in early so he could work on a special project and left at the end of the day wondering why he never got around to it? What happened to Paul is all too common: He had no real plan for the day, just a vague sort of hope, and therefore he had no basis for resisting the demands or requests of others and no psychological defense against his own tendencies to procrastinate. Paul is an example of someone who's ignored an important lesson: If you do not plan your day, other people will "plan" it for you; *their* actions will determine *your* priorities.

Planning goals and priority tasks for the day is the most important activity in time management. And to make sure the planning sticks, you must *write it down*. A written daily plan is your essential tool. With it, you are in control of your time. Without it, your days will be a frustrating jumble of minor crises, interruptions, and dead ends.

A daily plan will guarantee that you get your top-priority tasks done; guide you in determining the priorities of new tasks that arise during the day; give you psychological backup for resisting interruptions; tell you what to return to if you do get interrupted. Yet many, many people resist having one. Here are some typical reasons:

"Planning takes too much time." Actually, planning *saves* time. An hour spent in effective planning will save you three or four hours in execution—and give better results.

"I've been pretty successful so far without planning." You've been successful *in spite of* not planning. Planned results will always be more successful than chance results, other things being equal.

"Planning is too abstract; I need to get things *done*." Taking action without thinking things through is a prime source of problems. Those who know what to do may succeed once; those who know why, will succeed again and again.

"There's no point in planning; something is bound to come up, and then my plan is out the window." With planning, most emergencies can be prevented or defused.

First Things First

The key to successful time management is doing the most important task first, and giving it your full concentration, to the exclusion of everything else. The significance of the daily plan is that it forces you to do exactly that. This is planning at its core: Set priorities for the day, and then do the first one first. And that means *first*. Not after checking the mail, not after reading the daily paper, not after clearing away small jobs.

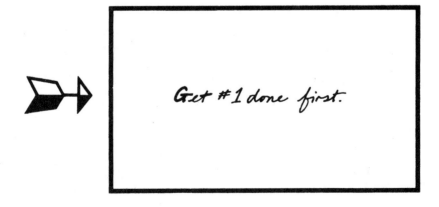

Get #1 done first.

It's such a simple idea, and yet so very hard to do. We're all human, and there is a strong urge for instant gratification. We crave the feeling of success, of having accomplished something definite, and so we want to start our day with a task that's easy and quick.

Does this sound familiar? "I'll just clear my desk first, so I'll have some room to work." Then, as you start sorting through files and papers you come across items from previous days that have not been completed. "Heavens," you tell yourself, "I didn't realize this hadn't been done; I'd better just clear this up first." It isn't nearly as important as what you should be working on, but it's easier, or more fun. And pretty soon you have, in Peter Drucker's wonderful phrase, "drifted into trivia." Instead of majoring in your main priorities, you begin majoring in minors. Your best energy is frittered away on minor tasks, and by the time you get to your top jobs, you are too tired to perform well.

A study I conducted at a major corporation revealed that, on average, managers did not get to their main task until midafternoon. How much more productive might they have been if they had started it first, instead of letting human nature pull them toward the insignificant?

If you make just this one change, you will see profound improvements in your use of time. Watch for these four immediate benefits:

1. You will be doing the most important task when you are at your best, and therefore you can do a better job.
2. The rest of the day is downhill.
3. When working on your top priority it's much easier to resist interruptions because few if any of them will be as important.
4. Even if nothing else in your plan gets done because of unexpected problems, you can leave at the end of the day with a feeling of having accomplished your top priority—with a clear conscience.

A Planning System

It's important to keep daily planning in perspective. No one is suggesting that you operate one day at a time. A daily plan is the basic tool, but it works best as an integral part of a larger system. The system I recommend has these five components, which interlock and work together:

1. *Objectives.* For significant personal and professional long-range goals, shorter-range objectives are set and planned a year at a time, including timelines. Progress is measured monthly.
2. *Project plan.* Major projects are timelined, with key dates and checkpoints noted. Progress is measured weekly.
3. *Monthly plan.* Project checkpoint dates and deadlines for objectives that fall within the month are noted, along with known appointments, travel plans, scheduled meetings, and so forth. Eighteen months are allotted to ensure adequate forward planning at the end of the year.
4. *Daily plan.* Do a week's worth at a time. Project dates that fall within the week are transferred, along with other appointments, from the monthly plan. Each day is divided into three segments for Goals, Appointments, and To Do's.
5. *Contact logs.* Provide separate sheets to record important communications with key individuals for instant retrieval when needed.

In my own work these various components are physically recorded in a planner/organizer system called Time Tactics, which I developed. This is of course not the only system available; in this chapter I will show you two other plan formats, and many others are possible. You may wish to make up your own format. The important thing is that you *do* it. Use a system in which you can record everything you must do or remember.

Your Daily Plan

This is where all the pieces come together, where goals turn into reality. Today is the time when something gets done, or not done; it can't be yesterday, and there are no guarantees about tomorrow.

The daily plan format I recommend (see Figure 5) has three parts:

1. Goals for the day—the two, three, four, or five tasks that you *must* get done
2. Scheduled appointments, meetings, blocks of time set aside for specific tasks
3. To-do list—things you don't want to forget; lower-priority tasks you hope to get done

Set Goals for the Day

List the tasks that are essential for today. These are the "musts"—any portion of a major project that is due today, an assignment from your boss, a critical report, and so on. At least one of these should be an activity that advances one of your own long-range goals. Others will derive from the company's long-range plans and your boss's goals and priorities.

Then rank them in priority order. Number one, remember, is what you're going to tackle first. Refresh yourself on the process of setting priorities, if needed; check the priority matrix in Chapter Three. Next, give yourself a deadline for achieving today's goals; set a time by when you plan to have completed each one. This will keep you on track as the day progresses. It will also provide reasons for saying no to interruptions, when warranted, because you'll always have deadlines coming up to which you can refer.

Schedule Appointments

All the day's timed activities are noted: meetings, one-on-one conferences, callbacks, appointments outside the building, luncheons, and so on. Some have been scheduled previously, some come through interaction with others during the course of the day. Written and spoken words continually shape and change the daily plan.

Also note blocks of time you have set aside for accomplishing specific tasks. This is where your ideal day (see Chapter Three) comes in. With it you will ensure that you work on activi-

Figure 5. Sample daily/weekly plan, sheet A.

February Week 8					199_2_
Monday 17 Washington's Birthday	**Tuesday 18**	**Wednesday 19**	**Thursday 20**	**Friday 21**	**Saturday 22**
Goals	Goals	Goals	Goals	Goals	Goals
1 Draft Video Costs	1. Slides	1. Review Pkg in-house	1. Final Draft Video	1. Graphics proposal	8:00 Sam tennis
2. Agenda Staff Mtg	2. Bank	2. Simo proposal			
3. Nevins Proposal	3. Correspondence		2. Weekly Appraisal	2. Nevins 1st draft	
	3. Final Draft	3. Nevins quote			
Appointments	Appointments	Appointments	Appointments	Appointments	
8:00 A.M.	8:00 A.M.	8:00 A.M.	8:00 A.M.	8:00 A.M.	
9:00 Tom—Accounting	9:00 Meet w/ Sue	9:00 KK proposal	9:00 no appts.	9:00 no appts.	
10:00	10:00 Staff Meeting	10:00	10:00	10:00	
11:00	11:00	11:00	11:00	11:00	10:00 Shopping—Len
12:00 P.M. Nevins Eatery	12:00 P.M.	12:00 P.M.	12:00 P.M. Sam at Tod's	12:00 P.M.	
		12:30 Rotary lunch			
1:00	1:00 Review Slides	1:00	1:00	1:00	
2:00	2:00	2:00 Marry—Printing	2:00	2:00 ck/Harry Slides	

3:00	3:00 Tom-Presents two	3:00 Finish Nevins grts	3:00 Review with Tom	3:00 Nevins 1st draft ✓	8:00 Tenant's party
4:00 Agenda to Typing	4:00 Final Draft	4:00	4:00 meet with Gene	4:00	Sunday 23
5:00	5:00	5:00	5:00 Weekly Appraisal	5:00	Set VCR Chan 13 10 pm
6:00	6:00	6:00 Cocktails — Sims	6:00 ✓	6:00	Review Nevins
7:00	7:00	7:00	7:00	7:00	
To do	To do	To do	To do	To do	
Jim — Editing Calls: 7B.	Order Dennis cake		Pop lunch w/ Sam; figures or proposal Needs list	Stop on way home for Len	
Checkout Collins	list of new Staff				
Call Game-at-fg Vue-it Sam	Sims-555-1212 —12 Park			Set meeting for next week	
Read Question article — Read Mktg Report	The Eatery 705 4th 8 p.m.		How many answers to ad?		

ties and recurring tasks at the same time every day—the time that is most convenient for you.

One very important block to schedule is an early meeting with your assistant to go over the outline of the day and plan strategy for accomplishing critical items. Another important block is the quiet hour.

Include a Quiet Hour

The quiet hour is one of the most successful and profitable time management techniques ever devised. For one hour a day, no phone calls, no visitors, no chit-chat, no interruptions of any kind—just quiet, uninterrupted work. Your assistant fields all calls and visitors, and takes messages for callbacks.

Almost without exception, everyone who has tried a quiet hour supports the idea enthusiastically. The only problem I have heard reported is that occasionally some people make self-conscious jokes in the beginning; many companies use the term "planning hour" to minimize this.

The results? On average, a person gets done in one quiet hour what would take three "normal" hours. Talk about productivity improvement!

The quiet hour works best if all in the organization participate. And all should have their quiet hours at the same time. If various departments or people set different hours, it's simply too difficult for everyone to remember which one has which hours, and the process breaks down.

What's the best time for the quiet hour? First thing in the morning, before the tempo of calls and meetings is up to speed.

Should there be any exceptions? As few as possible. Every exception lessens the overall effectiveness for everyone. Even those who insist that exceptions be made for them because they need access at all times usually change their minds once they see how much they can accomplish in their own quiet hour.

Keep a To-Do List

This is a catching place in your daily plan for noting items that come up during the day that you would like to get done but that have lower priority. Some may be personal or family tasks. Some may be carried over from yesterday, or even last week. Some could be lower-level action items that have no particular time frame. This list is a part of your daily plan, not a separate piece of paper that is easily lost. New time management systems have rendered the pocket diary and separate to-do list obsolete.

Stick to Your Plan

Put the day's goals and their deadlines someplace where they are visible all day long. This list is your primary tool for staying on track. If by 9:30 you can see you haven't made much progress toward your 10:00 deadline, you know what you have to do.

As mentioned above, the plan is also your main defense against interruptions. When someone asks for a "few minutes" of your time, look at your daily deadlines and see whether you have a few minutes to give away. When a telephone call about next month's shipping schedule shows signs of being a lengthy one, you'll know whether you can take the time to solve the problem now or whether you must postpone the call. When your boss asks you to do a rush job, you can tell in an instant whether doing it will jeopardize other priorities of his on which you are working.

But suppose it does? What then? Your daily plan is your strongest ally here: You can tell your boss what you are currently working on, and ask *the boss* to decide whether the new assignment is more important. Turn to Time Topic 4 for an example of what to say in this situation, to get the boss to determine the priorities of your work. That way, you're off the hook.

The Plan Sheet Format

A few years back I was introduced to the weekly plan sheet that is the core of the executive time management system used at Economics Laboratory in St. Paul, Minnesota. The senior managers of this organization were unanimous in their praise of the system. "No two managers use it the same way," one told me, "but I don't know of a single one who does not use the basic principles in one way or another. The concepts have penetrated our company so completely that it would be impossible to calculate its benefit."

The plan sheet (see Figure 6) provides an overview of a week at a time. It groups items into general categories: phoning, writing, general meetings, and lunches, and a separate page lists the key colleagues each person works with. Under the colleagues' names, each manager keeps a running tally of the topics to be discussed.

Items listed in all categories are designated a priority ranking, and those are tackled first. Thus, if a meeting with a colleague has to be brief, only the top one or two items will be covered.

The plan sheet works hand in hand with an appointment calendar. During the last hour of the day, managers review what was accomplished and organize the main activities for the coming day. At Economics Laboratory, by mutual agreement, no meetings are scheduled before 10 A.M. and the first hour—the quiet hour—is reserved for whatever each manager wishes to concentrate on.

The plan sheet concept has been adapted by the president of a small New England college, with outstanding results. You will recognize in Figure 7 many features of the previous plan sheet: regular blocks of time for categories of activities, items to discuss with key managers grouped under their names, and priority rankings assigned.

You are encouraged to experiment with various formats and see what works best; you may want to blend elements into your own custom design. The format of your daily plan is not important; the concept is vital.

Benefits of a Daily Plan

As a kind of summary, review these benefits that making and using a daily plan will provide:

1. Greatly reduces the number of decisions on "what to do next."
2. Minimizes interruptions and improves quality of work.

Figure 6. Sample plan, sheet B.

Phone

1 ✓ EBO lunch Fri.?
4 ✓ Greg—travel plans
KMM—Re Moving policy
Ross—Friday store visits O.K.
3 ✓ JMH—90-day travel plans
RWP/TMO R&D coordination
✓ Lunch Mon.—JMH

Lunch

Fri 7/12 Hideaway
Mon 7/15 JMH
Tues. 7/16 JJK
Wed. 7/17
Thurs. 7/18
Fri. 7/19 EBO
Mon. 7/22 St. Paul—GKC
Tues. 7/23 St. Paul—JAL
Wed. 7/24 St. Paul—KMM
Thurs. 7/25 St. Paul—M.M. meeting
Fri. 7/26 A.M. (Tentative)

Correspondence

5 ✓ Send EB info on December meeting—cc: FTL
JMH—competition raising quantity discounts?
Send FTL copy of Acquisition Screen

General

Finalize acquisition screen
Sales meeting agenda
Do linear charts for division by title

Secretary

2 ✓ Digest for St. Paul
Need acquisition screen file

(continued)

Figure 6. Continued.

EBO

Acquisition plans
Division strategy document (D)
linear charts by title
New Finish package design (D)
marketing Plans review dates

FTL

Division Strategy document (D)
city desk consolidation
Progress report schedule (D)
Attendance at national sales meeting
New finish creative strategy
marketing plans review dates

JMH

Review past / Future six month plans
Need to revise coverage control cards
Regional managers sales coverage on Star
6a 90-day travel plans (D)
✓ consumer field — regional expense control
Regional managers meeting — analyze all reports
Regional office executive development meetings

JJK 1 Status new advertising copy
Job standards (D)
2 military marketing plan
6b4 90-day travel plans
Status Trendex report
3 Cost Sam I — 3 test markets
Products on Bonus Program (D)
6 Nielsen coupon handling charges
5 Organization charts — review (D)

Figure 7. Sample plan, sheet C.

Week: _May 13_

Morning
8:30 - Evaluation
9:00 - Dictation
9:30 - Phoning
10:00 - meetings

Afternoon
1:30 - Phoning
2:00 - Meetings
4:00 - Miscellaneous

Lunches
Mon. _Faculty Committee_
Tues. _Rotary_
Wed. _Student Assn. offices_
Thurs. _____
Fri. _Trustee Richardson_

	Phoning	Writing	Meetings
Mon.	J. Brown	Board Newsletter	Administrative Council
	H. Williams	Gift Receipts	Budget Review Comm.
	Dr. Jones	(Key Donors)	75th Anniversary Comm.
	M. Wilson	Foundation Proposal	Faculty Mtgs.
	Univ. R.I.	Review	Dean of Students
Tues.	L. Buck	Bulletin Editorial	
	T. Mallion		
	R. Helms		
Wed.	R. Vicks		
	T. Freiburg		

General
Mortgage Negotiation
1991-92 Budget
Donor Calls
Foundation Call
Five year Projection

Thurs.	Univ. Club	
	H. Shaw	
Fri.	New York Visits for May 20-21	

(continued)

Figure 7. *Continued.*

Items for Discussion	Week: **May 13**

Dean of Faculty:

Priority	Subject
1	Report to board – 5/25
3	New Faculty Appointment
2	Summer Institutes
4	Plans for Library

Business Manager:

Priority	Subject
2	Board Financial Statement 5/25
5	April Computer Printout
8	Sale of Kenyon
1	Cash Flow → 6/30
3	New Secretary – Development
4	Mortgage Negotiation Early childhood Center
6	Budget Plan 1991–92
7	Summer Vacation Schedule

Dean of Students:

Priority	Subject
1	Exit Interview for Seniors
3	Personnel – Summer Plans
2	Financial Aid Policy review

Director of Development:

Priority	Subject
3	Alumni Fund Drive
1	New Secretary
4	Trustee Fund Drive
5	Budget for 91–92 (Dept.)
2	Income projections for 1991–92

Director of Admissions:

Priority	Subject
1	Status of Admissions application + finals
3	New brochure
4	Advertising 1991–92
2	Letters to new Students

Director of Communications:

Priority	Subject
1	Final Newsletter 6/91
3	Budget for 1991–92
4	New logo for college
5	Mailing list
2	25th Anniversary Plans

Priorities and deadlines for time segments serve as reasons for not allowing interruptions for less important matters.

3. Increases quantity of output—productivity and likelihood of accomplishing your most important priorities. In one quiet hour, you can accomplish what would otherwise take three hours.
4. Reduces "busyness" syndrome. Goals are visible, so they are not forgotten.
5. Reduces reactive syndrome. Instead of continually reacting to events and demands of others, you will be driven by your own priorities.
6. Replaces management by crisis with a sense of control. As your priorities are achieved, crises diminish.

Check Yourself

How successful are you at planning? Rank yourself on the following; then do it again three months from now.

Almost never	=	0
Sometimes	=	1
Half the time	=	2
Usually	=	3
Almost always	=	4

Points

1. I know the objectives, priorities, and plans of my organization. _____
2. I translate these objectives into monthly, weekly, and daily goals. _____
3. I keep these goals visible and measure my progress against them. _____
4. When priorities are in conflict, as in interruptions, I refer to my priorities for the day so I can make a rational decision on which priority should take precedence. _____
5. Priorities are agreed upon, understood, and communicated within my working unit. _____

Total _____

Attempting Too Much

The ways in which we manage ourselves and our time (for better or worse), our own particular set of work habits and personal idiosyncracies, are tangled up in a complicated kaleidoscope of interconnecting causalities. One time habit is linked with another, and when it shifts slightly, it has an effect on yet another.

This interlock phenomenon begins to show itself with our fourth time concern, attempting too much. Earlier we looked at the process of setting goals, and using those goals to establish priorities and plan your days around them. Without goals, priorities, and planning, you are leaving the future to chance. And you may be forced to pay the price sooner than you think. If you have not identified your ultimate target, you cannot know which interim objectives to set. Therefore, on any given day your priorities are either nonexistent or hopelessly confused. Without priorities you will tend to react to whatever comes by. You respond to the requests of others without passing them through the filter of your objectives or those of your organization.

Now comes the time trap of attempting too much. With no priorities to help you discriminate between the truly important and the not-so-important, you believe that *everything* has to be done. This creates a burden that, for some people, becomes unbearable.

The cost of attempting too much can be seen strewn across

the desks of disorganized managers. They don't have time to get organized. Deadlines are missed; pressure builds. Firefighting and crisis management become a way of life. They try to delegate but don't take the time to do it properly, so projects backfire. They foul up the work of others who depend on them for information. They work late but never seem to catch up. Their families accuse them of being workaholics, and they don't know what to say in defense.

In recent years, women have often been the victim of this particular trap. We even have a phrase for it: "the superwoman syndrome." While maintaining the perfect home, being the perfect hostess, partner, and mother, the superwoman must compete at work with male counterparts who have the advantage of more experience, a network of advocates and supporters, and rampant favoritism. So she must work twice as hard to reach the same level, where she will generally be paid two-thirds as much. Dr. Julia Files of the Mayo Clinic has addressed this problem in detail in her study of women's health issues and has concluded that the problem is just as severe now as it ever was.

Wouldn't women, and everyone else who is tempted to take on too much, be better off if they learned to work smarter, not harder?

A Tale of Two Salespeople

Not long ago a very successful and very hardworking salesperson showed up in a time management workshop (I think she had a little encouragement from her husband, and maybe her boss too.) For years she had worked from 7 A.M. until 7 P.M.—and went home feeling guilty about all the work she was leaving behind. But once she learned the principles of setting priorities, she began to practice them conscientiously. Not too long after the workshop, she looked up from her desk at 5 P.M. and saw that her staff was leaving for the day. She looked at her own daily plan, saw that she had accomplished five of the six daily goals, and said to herself, "That's good enough." She started to put job number six in her briefcase—then stopped herself. "Why am I doing this? It's the lowest priority; it can wait."

When she arrived home—on time, minus briefcase—her husband worriedly asked, "What's wrong?"

"Absolutely nothing. Everything's great. In fact, why don't we go out for dinner?"

And so they did, and enjoyed a wonderful evening together. Recounting this story, she told me she felt better that evening than she had in years.

The second story does not have a happy ending. A friend of mine was president of the National Association of Life Underwriters in a European country. It was a very demanding position, and it took most of his time—including time he should have devoted to his work. He enjoyed the attention and recognition of the presidency, but he looked forward to the end of his tenure so he could get back to his neglected business full time.

However, when the time came to elect a new president for the following term, no strong candidate emerged. Friends prevailed upon him to serve another term. Appealing to his loyalty—and his ego—they pleaded that only he could "save the organization." Against his better judgment, he accepted the draft. Too late, he realized that he was attempting too much. His business, already declining from neglect, fell completely apart. In the end, he was forced to give everything up and start over in another field.

Causes and Solutions

My friend's failing was overconfidence. This is the root cause of attempting too much—a sense that "I can do it all." It may not be visible, but this sense that you can accomplish whatever you decide to take on is at the heart of more obvious symptoms. Related causes include:

- The need to achieve, which leads us to take on more than we should.
- Insecurity, which keeps us striving to prove our worth.
- Failure to delegate authority, or lack of delegation skills.
- Unrealistic time estimates, resulting in planning too much for the time available.

- Not knowing how to say no, and a desire to please.
- Lack of personal organizational skills; the piles on your desk seem to grow geometrically when you're working on too many projects.
- Perfectionism, which leads us to unnecessary repetition and foolish investment in detail.

Some of these are particularly troublesome, and deserve our attention.

Learn to Delegate

The surest road to attempting too much is failure to delegate. For whatever reason—we don't think our staff can handle the job, we secretly think we could do better, we need to feel in control—many of us are reluctant to turn important jobs over to others. It may be understandable, but it is fatal. If you take on more and more because you think no one else can handle it, you will surely drown. Your boss is not going to be impressed that you have fourteen things on your agenda if you make serious mistakes in twelve of them.

If you are attempting too much because of inability to delegate, turn to Time Topic 6 and learn how to do it.

Learn to Say No to the Boss

Many people attempt too many tasks because they valiantly try to do everything the boss assigns to them. They need to learn how to say no to overloading. Almost every boss would prefer to have fewer things done well (especially if those things are the top priorities) than many things done sloppily.

If this has happened to you, you must explain your current work load, point out that you are working on these projects *for the boss,* and ask the boss to decide the priorities. You are managing your work by the boss's priorities—and that is the smartest thing you can do.

Let's say your boss calls you in and gives you two new projects to complete today. You say, "Okay . . . but can I ask a question first?"

If someone else drops the ball, do you really have to pick it up?

Any boss is going to assent to a question. Then you say, "I'm not sure if you are aware of it, but I have two other deadlines for you today, and I'm working on them right now. I know it's not possible to do everything, and I'm not sure which to do first—those two, or the two new ones."

In all likelihood he has forgotten what you're working on, and will appreciate the opportunity to step in here. Then you're off the hook. But what if your boss, in a flash of ill humor, says, "I want you to do them all." Assuming you have a reasonably good relationship with him, continue to stress your point:

"Well, I'll do my best, but I just can't guarantee that they'll all get done. I could guarantee the original assignments, but frankly, I have my doubts about the new ones. That's why I was hoping you would help me set the priorities. If something has to move over to tomorrow, I would hate to pick the wrong thing. So, I really do think it would be helpful for both of us if you could let me know which *you* think is the most important." No matter what your boss says at this point, you have put him on notice that finishing all the assignments is unlikely.

Learn to Estimate Time Better

Sometimes people get in trouble taking on too much because of unrealistic estimates about how long various jobs will take. This may be another facet of overconfidence—"I'm a fast worker; I can do it"—or it may be simple inability to estimate accurately.

Remember Murphy's Second Law: "Everything takes longer than you think." The solution here is to give yourself a cushion. Take your estimate and increase it at least 20 percent—more for very complex jobs or very critical ones. If you can relate this job to something similar in the past, use that experience to guide you in deciding on the amount of cushion.

How to Stop Attempting Too Much

If you frequently find yourself trying to do too much, how do you stop? Try these ideas:

- Stop telling yourself you work best under pressure; *nobody* works best under pressure.
- Resist the urge to step in and take over because others are not doing their job; their work is their responsibility, not yours.
- Don't assume that everything has to be done; learn to discriminate low-priority work . . . and ignore it whenever possible.
- Ask yourself if part of the problem is lack of organizational skills.
- Stop trying to make everything perfect; some things are simply not worth the extra effort.

Check Yourself

How successful are you at managing overload? Rank yourself on the following; then do it again three months from now.

Almost never	=	0
Sometimes	=	1
Half the time	=	2
Usually	=	3
Almost always	=	4

Points

1. When questions of overload arise for myself and my team members, I look first at how effectively the person is working.   _____

2. I practice saying no to low-value or otherwise inappropriate requests.   _____

3. I look for the inability to say no to the boss and practice the various techniques for asserting myself when appropriate.   _____

4. I set realistic time estimates on tasks.   _____

5. When facing overload situations, I examine the question of personal organization and take steps to ensure that it is not the cause.   _____

                                                Total   _____

Drop-In Visitors

"Hi. Got a minute?" A relatively innocent question, and one you probably hear several times a day.

"Sure. Come on in." Is this your automatic response? If so, you're not alone; 99 percent of us say that completely automatically. But you are setting yourself up for trouble, because you are allowing yourself to be interrupted—even *inviting* interruptions—without exploring alternatives. You are giving away control over your time to whomever happens to be asking for it!

Drop-in visitors are one our biggest time wasters because they are so common, and so hard to resist. It might be a friend, stopping by for a quick chat. It might be one of your team, needing information, advice, or a decision from you. It might be your boss, requesting an update on the project. It might be another manager, a colleague, asking for a favor. It might be a senior-level manager, needing research material from your department. The one thing they have in common is that they all demand, in one way or another, that you stop what you are doing and shift your attention to them.

Two things we know for certain: It will undoubtedly take longer than a minute (the average drop-in visit lasts ten minutes), and the time needed to recover your concentration and your momentum is longer than the actual time consumed by the visit (some say three times as long).

Causes

Why do we find it so difficult to say no to drop-in visitors? Human nature comes into the picture here. We all want to be needed, to feel important, and to be helpful, and all these psychological needs are tapped by that one innocent question. But if you surrender your time to another person because you want to be helpful, you'll inevitably create stress for yourself. And that's not all. You are depriving the organization of more important contributions you could be making if you weren't accepting needless interruptions. What's more, you may be depriving the interrupter of the challenge of having to figure out the answers—a significant learning experience.

What to Say to Visitors?

To control drop-in visitors, you must first find out, as specifically as possible, what's on their mind. Then, depending on the situation, do one of these four things:

1. Deal with their question (if it's truly brief or a genuine emergency).
2. Set up another time to meet with them.
3. Suggest they confer with another appropriate person.
4. Encourage them to work out a solution on their own.

Those are the four basic responses. But usually the problem is the more subtle one of not knowing what to say. We simply don't know how to deflect the interruption gracefully. When someone asks for "just a minute" of your time, but you really need to continue with what you're doing, try some of these responses.

Postpone:

Visitor: Got a minute?
You: Hi. What's up?
Visitor: Well, it's that Peterson case. I can't quite get a handle on it. Didn't you have something like this about a year ago?

You: Yeah. Judge Winston, ninth circuit.

Visitor: Can you tell me about it?

You: Sure. I think I have a few ideas for you. But right now I have to keep going on this brief. How about after lunch tomorrow?

With colleagues, there's no reason at all to be apologetic if you need to set up another time to talk. Demonstrate your good faith by putting it on your calendar right then.

Refer the visitor to someone else:

Visitor: Got a minute?

You: Actually, I'm really jammed. What do you need?

Visitor: There's some confusion about the architect's report, and she's out of town this week.

You: And. . . . ?

Visitor: And our proposal to the bank is due on Friday.

You: Well, I'm afraid I'm just not in a position to pull away right now. Check with Art; see if he can help. And let me know what you two work out.

Whenever possible, encourage your people to find their own answers. A good way to do that is to ask them questions:

"Who else have you asked for suggestions?"

"What answers have you come up with?"

"Why don't you decide what you think ought to be done and then see me in the morning?"

Schedule another time:

Visitor: Got a minute?

You: If it's really quick, maybe. What can I do for you?

Visitor: You had suggested I get some background information on the city council from you before I start on the press release.

You: Right, I did. Unfortunately, I have to finish this before the noon meeting, so we'll need to get together later. Is it just the city council stuff, or do you have more to go over?

Visitor: Just that.

You: Okay. I'd guess about fifteen minutes. How about 2:30 to-morrow?

When you reschedule a drop-in visitor, set a time limit. That way, both of you know how long to plan for, and your visitor won't be surprised when you end the meeting. If you're uncertain, never hesitate to ask.

> *You:* How long do you think it will take?
> *Visitor:* Half an hour, I guess.
> *You:* Well, that's going to be a problem for me this week; I've got some pretty tough deadlines. Do you think maybe we could cover the high spots in ten or fifteen minutes?

Answer the question:

On the other hand, if you can answer the question so briefly that your concentration is not broken, by all means do so. Then both of you can get on with your work.

> *Visitor:* Got a minute for a question?
> *You:* I'll try. What's the problem?
> *Visitor:* Do we have a policy on showing contact sheets to the client? They've asked several times, but the art director wants to wait.
> *You:* No, don't show them the contacts; just the final shot, and only when the whole ad has been designed.

Cut yourself short:

Frequently what you thought would be a quick question turns out to be more complicated. If after talking with your visitor for a few minutes, you can see the matter is going to take a while, say:

> Stephanie, you know, I thought this was going to be a short question, but I can see now that it's a little more than that. It's my fault; I should have asked you how long this was going to take. . . . I have this 10:00 deadline I've got to finish for my boss. Would you mind

if we put this off till tomorrow? Frankly, I don't think my mind will be on it right now.

Be candid:

Visitor: Got a minute?
You: Hi there, buddy. What's up?
Visitor: Nothing special. I've just been staring at those numbers all morning and need a break. How was the Alaska trip?
You: It was great. In fact, I've been wanting to get together and tell you all about it. Are you free for lunch?

With friends, you can be blunt if need be: "I hate to do this to you, but I just don't have the time right now; I hope you can understand."

Visiting for the sole purpose of socializing—and how you can control it—is discussed in Time Topic 15.

Whose Time Is More Important?

Another reason behind our difficulty with drop-in visitors is that we fail to see an interruption for what it really is: a conflict in priorities.

Let's look at a real-life example. You're gathering your notes and reviewing the agenda for your meeting at 11:00. At 10:45, an associate stops by your door and asks, "Do you have a minute?" Whatever is on his mind is his priority at that moment. But you have something else on your mind—getting ready for the meeting—and that is your priority. If you permit yourself to be interrupted, you are allowing his priority to take precedence over yours. If you refuse to be interrupted, then your priority has taken precedence over his.

In this particular case, you know that "a minute" to your associate means fifteen or twenty. Experience has taught you that his question usually can wait. Being late for a meeting you called would not be acceptable. You start to ask if this can wait, but your associate interrupts you with, "I've got to have the answer before noon and I know you won't be back by then." This associate often waits until the last minute to request information

> " Got a minute ? " never
> means just one minute.
> Before you say yes or no,
> always ask what it's about.

or decisions. Nevertheless, you turn back into your office saying, "Well, okay, but just a minute. My meeting starts at eleven and I can't be late."

As the associate's problem unfolds, several things become clear: It is a relatively low-priority matter and is not that urgent after all. He could have requested your input yesterday. Furthermore, he could have made the decision himself. Unfortunately, you are too far into the discussion to extricate yourself without embarrassment.

What did you do wrong, and how might you have handled this situation better?

• You seemed unable to say no. Lack of planning on the associate's part led to a late request for information, which, in turn, put you in a difficult situation. However, it also offered you a reason to decline the request by saying something like this: "If I'd known about this yesterday, I could have planned a little time for this discussion. Sorry, I can't take the time right now. Maybe tomorrow?"

• You started for the meeting late and left no time for a possible interruption or delay. Although it is best not to get into this trap, you could have controlled this situation by saying, "I've just enough time to make my meeting. I'm chairing it, so I just can't be late. I know you understand. Sorry."

• You failed to establish the priority of the problem before allowing the interruption. "What's it about?" is always a legitimate question and often a time-saving one.

- You did not explore alternative sources of answers for the questioner. In this situation, you might very legitimately have asked, "Have you tried Charlie?"

- You neglected to enforce the one-minute time limit suggested by the questioner. You should have extricated yourself when the requested time was up. "Sorry, I see our time is up. I really have to leave now. Maybe we can pick this up again when I return."

The Open Door

The problem of drop-in visitors has one other source, one that is to some degree dictated by others: the open-door policy. What started out as a good idea—make managers accessible to anyone with a legitimate need—has in many cases evolved into an open invitation for interruptions. In companies that have an open-door policy, many interpret it literally—and keep their doors wide open at all times. That open door seems to draw in idle gossipers as much as it does staffers with real questions.

The answer is to return to the original concept: Be available, *accessible,* to anyone who needs to see you. As for the door—the physical door—shut it! If your organization believes in enforcing the open-door policy literally, you and all your colleagues will have to exercise mutual respect, and make sure you remain extra sensitive to others' schedule needs.

Take care not to be an interrupter yourself. Keep a running list of items to discuss with key people, and bundle them into one meeting. Probably each person you see will have a few questions for you as well, and thus you don't interrupt one another five or six times a day.

Solutions

Screening. The macro solution to the problem of drop-in visitors is to have your assistant screen them, following the same four-part strategy as with screening telephone calls (see Time Topic 2):

1. First, handle the visitor if possible. If your assistant can provide the needed information, have him do so.
2. If he cannot answer the question, your assistant should try to refer the visitor to a more appropriate person.
3. If you are the only one who can answer the visitor's need, your assistant should schedule an appointment with you.
4. If the visitor is a VIP, or if the situation is an emergency, your assistant should interrupt you and show the visitor into your office.

To make the screening process work, see to it that your assistant's desk is placed near your office, so that visitors have to pass his desk on the way to your door.

"Hello, Mrs. Temple. Can I help you?"

"I need to see Frank. Is he busy?"

"He's working on the departmental budget for next year. Do you want me to interrupt him?"

Chances are, your visitor will say no. Then the assistant asks if he or someone else can help or, if not, offers to make an appointment with you.

You will find some people who resist the very idea of screening; they believe that appointments are only for outsiders. But a skillful, professional assistant can protect you from needless interruption without causing offense. It is your responsibility to back your assistant up in this; if an associate protests having to make an appointment to see you, say something like this: "I had asked Jim to help me carve out three uninterrupted hours so I could work on the president's speech. Now that I'm done with that, you have my full attention."

Schedule appointments for staff members. Establish a portion of the day when you will be available for anyone in your department or section who needs to see you, perhaps 10:00 to 3:00. Have your assistant schedule appointments within that block, and for a specific amount of time. Your visitor will simply have to request, "Please put me down for a half-hour with her sometime today." Your assistant should ask the purpose of the visit, so he can pull together background information for you.

Have your assistant monitor the visit. When the half-hour is up, he should interrupt you to remind you of your next appointment.

Extending that idea, some people set up regular "drop-in" hours; everyone in the organization knows they'll be available during that block of time, and saves questions until then.

Establish a quiet hour. The concept of a quiet hour is explained in Time Topic 3. When this very effective technique is used throughout the organization, productivity soars. Everyone knows that drop-in visits are forbidden during the quiet hour, for that time is set aside for uninterrupted concentration.

If you are unable to institute a quiet hour in the company, try your own department first. If that's unsuccessful, try putting a sign on your door: "QUIET HOUR. Please come back at 11:00." Some people come in an hour early each day. Before the phones start ringing and others start dropping in, you'll be surprised at how much you can accomplish. However, I recommend this as a last resort. If you come in an hour early, you should leave an hour early to compensate. No one should be forced to give up personal or family time to gain an atmosphere in which to think.

If you don't have an assistant. The strategies described above depend on your having a full-time assistant. If you do not—or if some visitor barrels around him—you'll have to use your own devices to limit visitor interruptions. Find out what the problem is, and how urgent it is; encourage people to find their own solutions or to call on other colleagues; set a specific time to get together later. Here are some other ideas:

- *Set a time limit at the beginning.* Say to your drop-in visitor, "Sure, I can help you with that. But I have to leave for a meeting at 10:15; do you think we can finish in fifteen minutes?" Since you don't have an assistant to monitor the visit, do it for yourself: Set your watch alarm.

- *Go to the other person's office.* You're much more in control when you're in the other person's office; you can leave whenever you're ready, rather than having to ease your visitor out of your office. So when someone drops in, find out what the problem is and then try something like this: "I need about ten minutes to wrap up this article; why don't I come down to your office then?"

• *Stand up.* This is an extremely effective technique for keeping visits short. When someone stops in "just for a minute," stand up to greet him. Find out what the question is, answer it if it's quick, or reschedule if you need to—all the while standing. Once you ask your visitor to have a seat, you're inviting him to stay a while.

Standing is also a way to bring an end to a conversation in which you and the other person are already seated. Stand up while smiling and speaking cordially—and move toward the door. The other will move with you.

• *Hide.* Find someplace in the building you can use as a hide-away—an unused conference room, an empty office, a corner of the library, the cafeteria at non-mealtimes. There are two benefits: No one can find you, so interruptions are cut to zero; and you will probably find the atmosphere in the unfamiliar surroundings more stimulating. In one company that I worked with, people had reached an agreement that whenever someone was out of the office for the day, anyone else could use his or her desk for concentrated work. Being at someone else's desk was an automatic signal that you were working intently and did not want to be interrupted.

• *Prevention.* With many people now self-employed, creative ways are being developed and accepted for balancing customer service needs with the need to avoid interruptions. For example, "drop-in" is being replaced by "drop off," in which business communications are routinely "dropped" in mailboxes or under doors, even though both people know the receiving party is physically present.

What About the Boss?

Don't be surprised if the got-a-minute person is your boss. If the visit comes at a particularly bad time, or if it seems to be more social than anything else, incorporate mention of your current projects for him or her as discreetly as you can, and as soon as you can. Make clear you are talking about deadlines you are working on *for the boss.* Ask if you can come to the boss's office later, so that other matters could be discussed at the same time. Ideally, work toward establishing a set time each day to get together, so that all items that have come up for either one of you can be dealt with.

Check Yourself

How successful are you at managing drop-in visitors? Rank yourself on the following ; then do it again three months from now.

Almost never	=	0
Sometimes	=	1
Half the time	=	2
Usually	=	3
Almost always	=	4

Points

1. My drop-in visitors are screened effectively. _____
2. Whenever possible, I complete tasks before permitting an interruption. _____
3. I time-limit interruptions whenever possible through my assistant, or myself if I do not have that kind of assistance. _____
4. Before accepting an interruption, I ask what it's about so I can assess its priority relative to my own. _____
5. Before proceeding with an interruption, I explore alternative solutions: What efforts, if any, has the interrupter made to solve the problem? Who else might be equally or better situated to help? Could postponing action be in everyone's best interests? What would happen if nothing were done? _____

Total _____

Ineffective 6 Delegation

After fourteen years with the company, Harry had recently been promoted to first-line supervisor. He was worried about the possibility of things going wrong, and so insisted that everything must cross his desk. The shop forepeople didn't like having to wait to get Harry's okay every step of the way; some were openly resentful. Orders were piling up; production was backlogged. Harry worked late every night, struggling to keep up.

Fortunately, Harry's section manager diagnosed the real problem: Harry felt responsible for *everything;* he was reluctant to delegate any responsibility. Harry's boss called him in and, with candor and genuine concern, pointed out that Harry's predecessor achieved excellent results and yet rarely worked overtime. The predecessor delegated everything possible to those who proved they could handle difficult assignments. Harry was in danger of losing his best workers by not giving them challenging tasks. Whenever he did work that he could have given to others, Harry was being overpaid.

Harry got the message. He met with each foreperson to talk about the tasks he or she would like to be given, delegated those tasks, and worked out a mutually agreeable system of progress reports. He's now going home on time.

Overcoming Reluctance to Delegate

Harry's situation is not unusual. Many managers have difficulty delegating work to their team members. There are several reasons for this, most of them having to do with human nature. Once we understand the source of this reluctance, we can work toward overcoming it.

- *Ego.* Nowhere is ego more evident than in this time waster. Most of us are vulnerable to thinking, "I could do it better." Ironically, we are also vulnerable to its opposite: "What if the person I give this to does a better job than me?"

In both cases, the solution is simple: Delegate it anyway. If someone on your team does an outstanding job on an assignment, the entire organization profits—and your reputation is not diminished in the slightest. And while it may be true that you could do the task better *this time,* you will be depriving your associate of an important learning experience.

- *Anxiety about mistakes.* This may be the biggest underlying cause: fear that the person who is given the assignment will blow it, and you will have to pick up the pieces—if indeed they *can* be picked up. As a manager you should create an atmosphere in which mistakes are tolerated. Little of value is accomplished where nothing is risked.

Part of the legend about Henry Ford concerns his way of handling mistakes. It is said that once a vice-president, who had made a mistake that cost the company $20 million, came to Henry with resignation in hand. "No way," Ford responded, "we've spent too much money educating you to lose you now."

- *Comfort level.* A very common problem is managers continuing to work at their prior job, because they are comfortable with that work; they know exactly how to do it, and exactly what it takes to succeed. The job of a manager can be fraught with anxiety, and there is a strong temptation to retreat to the more routine tasks that we already know how to do—even when those tasks should be delegated to someone else. So the design engineer who gets promoted to engineering manager still does circuit design, rather than managing the flow of work in the section. To succeed as a manager, you must move away from the work you currently know, and pay attention to the future.

• *Fear of losing control.* If you have done a good job in the delegation process, you will retain ultimate control; you and the worker will have agreed on a schedule of checkpoints and progress reports (see Time Topic 18), and you will know—in time to take action—if something goes awry.

This can be a real problem if your boss, for whatever reasons, likes to have a hand in everything. If asked for details on a project that you have delegated to someone else, say, "I've delegated that to Patricia. I'll be happy to check with her and get you the answer this afternoon."

• *Desire for perfection.* You can probably blame your parents for this one, if they taught you this rule: "If anything is worth doing, it's worth doing well." This, combined with your secret sense that no one can do it as well as you, compels you to keep the task for yourself, so that it can be done to your standards. Loosen up on this idea; it will lead you to overcontrol, and that leads ultimately to failure. Learn to accept reasonable, adequate work; learn to recognize perfectionism for the time waster it is.

• *Lack of confidence in others.* This concern is very understandable, especially if you are delegating a task to a person who has never done it before. You *should* be delegating; how else will anyone learn? Yet, you say, how can I trust the work will be done correctly? The solution is a leap of faith. Take the plunge, and assume that, with your support, the project will be accomplished satisfactorily. Acknowledge the risk involved, and take steps to minimize it: Give clear instructions, coach and counsel, and get regular progress reports.

• *False sense of efficiency.* Often managers decide not to delegate a job because "I can do this myself in half an hour; it would take Wendell two hours." (Sometimes this comes out as "It would probably take me longer to show someone how to do this than to go ahead and do it myself.") Both these statements may be true, but both completely miss the point. So what if it takes Wendell two hours to do the job? Next time, he can do it faster. More important, by giving the job away you have bought yourself an extra half hour. In that half hour you can do something that *only you* can do, something that would be far more valuable to the organization.

Steps in Effective Delegation

Every time you start to do something, ask yourself, "Could someone else do this?" If your answer is yes, delegate it! To ensure your associate does a good job, make sure *you* do a good job of delegating.

Choose the right person. We start with the assumption that you have qualified people on your team (if you think you don't, check the ideas in Time Topic 14), and that on your staff there are one or more people who can do the job. Make the best match you can between talent and task. Remember, though, that part of the purpose of delegation is education. Don't automatically reject a person with minimal experience in the particular kind of task; you'll be robbing him or her of valuable training.

Give clear instructions. Make it clear what you expect as a final product and any intermediate requirements. Define standards of what will constitute an acceptable job, and discuss them fully. Be thorough; explain all critical points. Ask the person to repeat, so you are sure that both of you understand things the same way.

Give commensurate authority. Assigning someone the responsibility for a task is one thing; giving them the authority to accomplish it is another. To be effective you can't do one without the other. Make sure the person has the authority to obtain whatever is needed to do the job—financial resources, clerical assistance, equipment, interdepartmental information, or anything else. For more on clear authority, see Time Topic 16.

Follow up. Work out a system of regular progress reports with the individual who will be doing the job. This will ensure that if anything goes off track, you will know it in time to make corrections.

Support and coach as needed. Throughout the project, make yourself available for questions, advice, or any other assistance that may be needed. Remember this is to be a learning experience; be a good teacher. At the same time, don't overcontrol. If your people feel you looking over their shoulders at every moment, their motivation, and their creativity, will shrink.

Resist upward delegation. This problem is sometimes also called "reverse delegation"—team members bringing to you the problems they themselves should be handling. This is especially easy to do with a boss who is tempted to think "I can do it better myself."

The core concept of delegation is appropriate decision level: Each decision should be made at the lowest possible level where the necessary facts are available and the required judgment exists. The higher in the organization a manager is, the more valuable her time—in sheer dollars and cents. If she makes a decision that someone on her staff could have made, she is wasting the company's investment in her.

The moral here is: Don't do your team members' work for them, even temporarily; you'll be cheating them (they miss the opportunity to learn), cheating your company (it misses good use of your talents), and cheating yourself (you have to work long hours to do it all).

How to Do It Right

The scenario described here contains many of the key points about good delegation.

Do *NOTHING* you can delegate.

The president of the company wants input from all divisions for the company's long-range marketing plan. Your boss, the division manager, has asked each department to produce a departmental draft plan. You decide to give the assignment to Pamela; although she has no specific background in marketing, she has a creative way of looking at problems and an orderly approach. But when you call her in, her first reaction is resistance.

"Oh, I don't think I can do that!"

"Well then, let's talk about this for a bit. Tell me, why don't you think so?"

"Because I've never done anything like it."

"Well, Pam, would it surprise you to know that that's the very reason I chose you for this job? It's going to be a wonderful learning experience. I know you can do a good job on this. I also know you have the intelligence to ask a question if you're uncertain about something. Don't worry, we're in this together. If I fail to give you the guidance you need, then that will be *my* fault. I'll be behind you every step of the way. So welcome to the vast army of all of us who've been given things we didn't think we could do. This is your number-one priority now, and you've got my total support. Let's get together to review your preliminary ideas on Friday."

How to Delegate When You Have No One to Delegate To

If you work in an organization, but have no one to delegate to, try trade-offs with your co-workers. Or simply ask for help and then reciprocate.

If you are independently employed, try forming (1) temporary alliances; (2) partnerships on a project-by-project basis; and (3) trading services. It's a good idea and a great time-saver to put these agreements down on paper. I've seen many such creative arrangements flourish on a smile and a handshake—and an equal number that floundered.

A Closing Thought

The essence of management is achieving objectives through the efforts of other people—in other words, delegating. A person who cannot delegate cannot manage.

Two key points to keep in mind about delegation: Do it (so you don't spend time doing things others could and should be doing) and do it right (so you don't have to spend time undoing a poor job).

Check Yourself

How successful are you at managing delegation? Rank yourself on the following; then do it again three months from now.

Almost never	= 0
Sometimes	= 1
Half the time	= 2
Usually	= 3
Almost always	= 4

Points

1. I assess the match between the task and the person to be delegated to. _____

2. I recognize that delegating a more difficult task than a person has done previously may be the best way to train that person. _____

3. To enhance motivation I offer support and counsel, without overcontrol. _____

4. I recognize reverse delegation when I see it and refuse to permit it. _____

5. I insist on regular progress reports on all major delegated tasks to ensure that problems will be detected in time to take corrective action. _____

Total _____

Personal Disorganization

Do you recognize this desk? A mountain of bulging file folders, some with their contents leaking out onto the desk or sliding into other piles. A flip-over daily calendar, open to yesterday. A stack of computer printouts, inventory records, and who knows what else. A coffee cup. A sheet from a lined yellow pad, "TO DO" boldly scrawled across the top, half buried by today's mail—still unopened. Random notes written on scraps of paper, napkins, and backs of envelopes. Three reference books, two with pencils sticking out of them. A pile of magazines, matched by three other piles on the credenza. Half-finished reports. Another coffee cup. Memos from others in the organization, little yellow tags sticking out in numerous places. And dozens of pink telephone message slips scattered over everything.

Would it surprise you if I told you the owner of that desk forgot an appointment today, lost an important document yesterday, and missed a deadline last week? Several times a day he searches through seven or eight stacks of papers, finding all sorts of letters, requests, reports, memos that need attention but not finding the one piece he is looking for—if indeed he remembers what it is.

It's easy to make jokes about being disorganized, but there is nothing funny about this kind of chaotic environment. Even less amusing is the half-hearted excuse: "I'm a creative kind of person; I have more important things to do than keep my desk organized."

Chronically disorganized people are a serious liability to their organization. They cannot be depended on to provide information to others: They forget where it is. They blow deadlines because they haven't written them down. They waste an enormous amount of time—theirs and other people's—searching for files, phone numbers, a contact's name. To compensate, they work longer hours but never seem to get caught up. And all too often others are sucked into the tornado, covering for the teammate who's still on yesterday's calendar page.

The overall solution to getting and staying organized is an integrated system, with a reliable place for all the pieces that are now scattered around your desk—and the self-discipline to stay with it.

Keep Your Desk Clean

Get rid of the notion that a loaded desk is the sign of a very busy, very important person. It's the sign of nothing but disorganization. One company president was asked why he had only one item on his desk. He responded that he had found that one important item was all he had to concentrate on at one time and that he was far more effective if he worked that way.

Your goal is to keep your desk clear of all except what you are working on at the moment. One thing at a time is enough for anybody to be working on. With two things, your mind switches back and forth between them. Three things, and you're totally lost.

Watch out for the common trap of keeping work on top of your desk "so I won't forget about it." You'll remember it, all right—it screams for attention all day long. Even when you're trying to work on Project A, every time your glance falls on the folder labeled Project B, your attention skitters over to it. And if Project C is peeking at you as well, you don't stand much of a chance of finishing A. You have to contend with enough interruptions from others, without interrupting yourself this way.

Rely on your daily plan to tell you which project you should be working on. Everything else must wait its turn—out of sight.

If you don't have an assistant, you may need an in-box to keep others from dropping papers on your desk during the day. If you do have an assistant, keep your in-box on *his* desk.

A small note of caution: Don't overdo it. Don't become so fastidious about your system that you cannot function if one sheet is out of place.

Toss the To-Do List

When people first start using a to-do list, they are mighty pleased with themselves. Gone are the odd bits of paper and reminders, the crumpled-up notes rescued from pockets, purses, and briefcases. Everything is written down, all in one place, never to be lost again. They feel in control, on top of things at last. And there is the wonderful sense of accomplishment as items are crossed off in bold, strong strokes.

It isn't long, however, before they begin to sense that something is wrong with their system. Maybe they have everything on one list, but they can't always *find* the list. Under pressure to write things down at a given instant, they start a new list. They don't have time to consolidate the two lists, so they keep both. Pretty soon one is left at home, another in the car, another in the briefcase.

Multiple to-do lists cause multiple headaches. There's the time wasted in duplicating records. There's the frustration of knowing something is listed somewhere—but where? And what was it, exactly? Inevitably, the same item appears on two lists. Then there's another frustration: It's crossed off on one list but not another. Was it done, or. . . . ?

Get rid of your to-do list; it's a handicap. Instead, use an integrated organizer system, in which you record all the items you have to remember, do, or plan for—in priority order, on the day you have to do them.

Use an Integrated System

All the individual tools of organization are worthless if there is no system for integrating them. You must find a way to make the tools work in concert with and reinforce one another. An organizer system—combining the features of a calendar, a diary, a to-do list, a personal phone directory, project control sheets, long-range planning sheets, and contact notations for action and followup—is the answer. The system can be maintained manually, on paper, or using any of a number of computer software packages, generically known as personal information managers. Either way, all the scattered pieces of your life are pulled together in one place.

The planner/organizer system I use is one I developed, called Time Tactics. It provides a place for:

- Daily goals, appointments, and lower-priority to do's
- Control sheets for tracking major projects
- Contact log, where key decisions and action items needing followup are recorded
- Individual dividers for contacts with key people I meet with regularly
- Monthly plans and long-range objectives
- Alphabetical directory

There are other excellent systems available; you may even enjoy working up your own customized program. Remember, a sound time management system must:

- *Be functional.* It must have a place for everything you have to do or remember, and it must all be instantly available for quick recording.
- *Provide retrievability.* Items must be recorded and placed where they can be retrieved quickly and easily, even if they were recorded months earlier.
- *Keep objectives and projects visible.* Long-range goals, short-range objectives, and checkpoints for projects must all be kept visible so they don't slip from your mind.

- *Keep deadlines visible.* Your deadlines will unfailingly keep you on track—as long as you don't lose sight of them.

Be sure that whatever system you select contains some type of contact log; this is what will keep you from getting buried in individual slips of paper—or, worse yet, losing one. For each phone call, each meeting, each encounter with another person, make a quick note of the key decisions reached and the action that should follow, both yours and the other person's. Three types of contacts will be recorded in order to speed retrieval: *key contacts* (people you deal with regularly, such as your assistant and your boss), *alphabetical contacts* (occasional contacts, such as a builder or a sales prospect where a series of contacts may be important for future reference), and *daily contacts* (other important contacts not fitting the first two categories). Some of these items will need to be transferred over to the appropriate spot on a daily plan as well. The contact log (see Figure 8) will be a chronological, running tally of the key points you should remember and all the details you'll need for followup. When one sheet is full, move to the next one; when all indicated actions have been taken, file the logs. By checking back through your log sheets at any time, you can retrieve an individual piece of information. Separate tabs are used for key contacts to speed recording and retrieval.

Computerized time management systems can keep track of appointments (some even give you audible reminders), file and index notes, look up telephone numbers and place calls, monitor progress of projects, and keep lists and schedules on a variety of topics.

Of course no system will work if you neglect to use it. The real key to effective use of a time management organizer is taking a few minutes each day to review what has been accomplished and plan for the next day.

Designate a Place for Today's Papers

Your time management organizer replaces the many separate pieces that used to clutter up your desk: calendar, to-do list,

Figure 8. Sample contact log.

Contact Log						
		Name _Dick Brown_ Company _Video Productions_				
Date	Priority	Item	When	Who	Action Taken	
1/8	1	Talked to DB (800-555-1100) about them givng us bid.				
		They'll send info. 3 days after they receive our spec				
		Asked Mary to send spec	1/9	Mary	mailed	
		Address: 50 Main St. Cityville, N.J. 00000				
		DB is tri-cities sales rep.				
		FR: ck their price goes into computer	1/20	Kim	on calendar	

and all those separate notes and jottings. The journals, reference books, and back reports have been put away. The files relating to projects you will tackle some other time are in your drawer or the file cabinet, waiting their turn. All that remains is the need for a system for the files and other material you will need to work with today.

The key is to have a place for every piece of paper you expect to use today. The best system I've seen is built around a set of colored folders. A few categories are set up, colors are assigned, and specific procedures for dealing with items in each category are established. A full example is shown in Figure 9.

These categories are generally useful: Urgent, Phone Call, Dictate, To Do, Review. Papers that pass over your desk are sorted (by your assistant, if you have one) and those that will be needed today are placed in the appropriate folders. Everything else is delegated to other people, filed for later review, or tossed.

Pulling It All Together

Coffee in hand, you're ready to start the day. Write down goals for today, rank them in priority order, and set deadlines for each. All projects, phone calls, correspondence, meetings, and appointments are listed on your daily plan or plan sheet in your planner/organizer. Organize the background files and correspondence you will need for today's projects. All other papers should be in their place (drawer or file cabinet) until you need them.

Start work on your number-one project for the day; stay with it until it's finished or taken as far as possible. Then put it away, and pull out number two. Periodically check the red folder; it has critical items.

When you hit the time in your day that you have set aside for phone calls, pull out the blue folder. During long phone calls, reach for the orange folder and sign today's correspondence. Check other noncritical action items in the folder: Is the one on top still the most important? When you hit the "dictation" time block on your daily plan, pull out the yellow folder. If you're

Figure 9. Sample procedures for handling work priorities.

Category	Items	Procedure
A. Urgent (Red folder)	A-1. VIP messages, callbacks, or deadlined requests.	A-1. Expedite/interrupt if necessary.
	A-2. Daily mail requiring same day attention.	A-2. Running summary stapled inside cover.
	A-3.	A-3.
B. Call (Blue folder)	B-1. All nonurgent calls.	B-1. All calls in blue folder with most important on top.
	B-2.	B-2. Running summary of calls stapled inside cover.
	B-3.	B-3.
C. Dictate (Yellow folder)	C-1. All nonurgent dictation.	C-1. Back correspondence attached if helpful.
	C-2.	C-2. Key requests underlined.
	C-3.	C-3. Running summary of letters, memos stapled inside folder.
	C-4.	C-4.
D. To Do (Orange folder)	D-1. Document/corres. ready for signature.	D-1. Page to sign on top or clearly marked.
	D-2. All action items not included above.	D-2. Fit into day whenever possible.
		D-3. Review at least weekly to prevent backlog.
		D-4. Ask what action to take.
		D-5. Keep running summary.
E. Review (Green folder)	E-1. All articles, memos, etc. of general but not urgent interest.	E-1. For trips, weekends, etc.

heading out for a trip, an appointment that might involve a wait, or home for the weekend, tuck the green folder in your briefcase.

As you complete projects, the related paperwork goes in a folder or box marked "file." You, or your assistant if you have one, will file these away according to a systematic procedure that ensures you can find things later. The full story on organizing sensible files is in Time Topic 12.

Electronic Aids

A number of electronic instruments can help you conquer personal disorganization: computers with astonishing speed and massive storage space, laptops or electronic "notebooks," software for managing your contacts, your projects, and your schedule—and personal digital "assistants" which fit easily into your pocket or can download from your computer into your wristwatch. But that is *all* these electronic marvels can do—help. Only you, applying the classic principles of time management and exercising the self-discipline addressed in Time Topic 8, can conquer personal disorganization on a daily basis for a lifetime.

Check Yourself

How successful are you at personal organization? Rank yourself on the following; then do it again three months from now.

Almost never	=	0
Sometimes	=	1
Half the time	=	2
Usually	=	3
Almost always	=	4

Points

1. I keep important tools within easy reach: planner/organizer, computer, working files, telephone, calculator, dictation machine, phone book. _____

Points

2. I ensure that my people have the resources needed to complete tasks on time.   _____

3. I recognize the distracting power of a cluttered desk and I practice keeping my desk clear of all but the task being worked on.   _____

4. I maintain a system for recording in one place everything I have to do or remember.   _____

5. I remove distractions, such as other work on my desk, before starting any task.   _____

6. I keep my work space organized in a system so that tasks may be accomplished in order of priority.   _____

Total   _____

Lack of Self-Discipline

Self-discipline is, of course, the key to making most of our time management techniques work. It takes discipline to stick with one important job until it is finished. It takes discipline to keep working when friends and colleagues are enjoying a social visit. It takes discipline to refrain from interrupting a co-worker to ask about a routine matter.

However, because lack of self-discipline causes sufficient difficulty on its own, the topic deserves separate attention.

Where Does the Problem Lie?

One cause of poor self-discipline is poor health or even simple fatigue. When you are not feeling your best, or are exhausted from working long hours and responding to the multiple demands on your time, you don't always have the mental and emotional energy to concentrate on the job at hand. If that is the case, make whatever changes are necessary to take care of yourself. Start an exercise program. Review your nutrition habits. Get some extra sleep; try going to bed an hour earlier. Leave your work in the office on Friday night, and take a mini-vacation this weekend.

Another source of this problem is lack of interest in the work. Indifference is a powerful demotivator. If you are bored or unchallenged, you will find it all the more difficult to exercise the discipline needed to work well. Examine your attitude toward your work, and honestly evaluate your situation: Is the problem with the work, or with you? What can you do to improve things? Perhaps ask your boss for a more challenging assignment? Offer to help co-workers? If you could better plan routine tasks so you could finish them faster, could you make room for other responsibilities? If your talents are underused at work, consider volunteering for a special project in a community organization. The feeling of accomplishment could energize you in other areas of your life, and provide the boost you need to recover enthusiasm about work (not to mention the good you will do for the organization).

Self-discipline is a habit, and lack of it is a habit too. Ask yourself a tough question: Is this a case of old-fashioned laziness? If it is, do you want to continue to see yourself as a lazy person?

One final source is lack of awareness. The question of self-discipline takes some people by surprise. They have been relatively successful thus far, and so have never had reason to think about it. Once they do, they realize that self-discipline could make them far *more* successful.

In addition to these direct causes of problems with self-discipline, the following links to other time concerns can be considered indirect causes:

- Lack of deadlines and priorities, which encourages putting things off and doing what we like rather than what we should
- Failure to follow up, which renders corrective discipline impossible
- Lack of challenging goals, which leads to lack of motivation

What Can Be Done?

A big part of the solution to self-discipline is self-talk. Stop saying, "I just don't have any self-discipline; it's just the way I am."

Stop saying, as you bounce around from one thing to another, "Well, I like to keep busy." Psych yourself up. Tell yourself, over and over, that you are an organized, orderly person and you have the discipline to do what needs to be done.

Develop the Habit of Self-Discipline

Act as though you were a self-disciplined person—and soon you will be. You'll be surprised how quickly habits form. A popular writing teacher in the Pacific Northwest encourages her students, most of them beginning writers with full-time responsibilities elsewhere, to do three things: (1) Think of themselves as writers; (2) write something every day; and (3) pick one place for writing, and don't do anything else there.

She tells a story on herself: As a struggling young writer without much furniture, she used a card table as her writing desk. One morning she sat down at that table to write a personal letter—and found herself still there six hours later. The habit of doing serious writing at that table was so strong that she had begun working on her novel without even realizing it. The moral to this story is: Once the habit is strong enough, the discipline is automatic.

Build In Reinforcement

As you enact your program of developing self-discipline, set up circumstances that will provide reinforcement:

1. *Keep goals visible.* Set goals and place them where you can see them all day. Whenever you are tempted to procrastinate or to dawdle, your goals will refocus you.

2. *Use all available tools.* Make sure you are taking advantage of all the tools: an organizer system, daily plan, project plan sheet, progress reports, timer for phone calls.

3. *Set deadlines.* Even if the project does not have a deadline, set one. Better yet, break it down into several steps and give each one a deadline. Nothing creates a sense of urgency like a deadline; it will force you to discipline yourself.

4. *Plan your activities, and establish priorities.* A daily plan, with tasks in priority order, will give you structure. Without a plan, you'll mentally wander around in a most undisciplined fashion.

5. *Make good time estimates and monitor progress.* Make regular progress reports to yourself. Are you where you planned to be? If not, use discipline to correct the course.

6. *Reward yourself.* Success should not go unnoted. When you complete a goal, give yourself a reward.

7. *Pick a hero for a model.* Our world is filled with stories of people who faced what appeared to be impossible challenges and, with strong will, overcame them. Thomas Edison discovered rubber after 1,500 experiments—which means he had 1,499 failures and still kept going. Glenn Cunningham, former world-record track star, was burned so badly as a child that doctors said he would never walk again. Werner von Braun failed the first course in mathematics he ever took; he accepted that failure as a challenge and vowed to master the subject.

Disciplined people have common characteristics. They don't settle for "almost," and they don't give up. They set tough targets for themselves and keep going until they reach them. Then they set even higher goals.

Check Yourself

How successful are you at self-discipline? Rank yourself on the following; then do it again three months from now.

Almost never	=	0
Sometimes	=	1
Half the time	=	2
Usually	=	3
Almost always	=	4

Points

1. I develop a plan with clear goals each day and I keep it visible at all times. _____
2. I set deadlines for every major task for myself and my team. _____

Points

3. I require regular progress reports on all deadlined tasks. _____
4. I check progress against my daily deadlines. _____
5. I refrain from interrupting others on matters that can wait. _____

Total _____

Inability to Say No

It has been said that the strongest time management tool in the world is one tiny, two-letter word: *no*. I'm not sure I agree that it is *the* strongest tool, but it is certainly near the top.

There are dozens of reasons why people have difficulty saying no to requests from others, but the results are always the same: overload, overtime, and overstress. The person who cannot say no seems perpetually to be shrinking, getting smaller and smaller behind a mountain of work that is always getting bigger and bigger.

Let's stop here and draw a distinction between the problem of attempting too much (Time Topic 4) and the inability to say no. Those who attempt too much suffer from overconfidence; they *think* they can do everything. Inability to say no means not knowing how, not having the emotional fortitude to refuse. Timidity, or need to please, or fear of offending, or similar emotion-driven impulses lead people to say yes to all requests.

The best approach to curing your habit of automatically saying yes, even when you don't want to, is to review the underlying reasons. An inordinate desire to please, to win approval, heads the list. Wanting to please is one thing; most of us are people-pleasers at heart. Indeed, the humanitarian instinct to help those in need is a worthy trait. But wanting to please so badly that you lose sight of your own priorities is something else.

If you possess talents or capabilities that are in high demand in your organization, the ability to say no will be especially important. Without it, you can easily fall victim to others who need your services, and soon you will have no time for your own work. Ego is a real trap here. The need to feel needed, important, valuable can easily lead you into taking on more than you can handle. After a while, your "askers" will figure out that they can take advantage of you.

A number of people fall into saying yes when others refuse to accept responsibility; they step in to fill the void. This is admirable within limits, but can lead to martyrdom. Too often those who give their all for the cause are expected to continue doing so. Learn to draw the line.

Inability to say no includes saying no in an ineffective way—hesitantly, apologetically, self-deprecatingly. Timid no-sayers usually start with an excuse, in a weak attempt to work up to saying no:

"Well, gee, I don't know. I've got so many other things to do. . . ."

The trouble is, the person making the request has usually anticipated every possible excuse and has prepared a rebuttal. Recognize this one? "Oh I know you're busy, that's exactly why we chose you! If you have a tough job, you go to people who are busy because they get things done." If you give a half-hearted no, you are encouraging the requester to think you can be talked into it. By presenting weak excuses, you are building false hopes.

Do you have to say yes if you can't think of a strong excuse? Absolutely not! You don't need an excuse. If you decide to say no to a request, you do not have to justify your decision if it is inappropriate for the requester to know your reasons. Simply say, "I'm sorry, but I'll have to say no this time."

Requests that come without warning are especially difficult. You can't quickly think of a reason to say no, so you say yes instead. In this situation, all the odds favor the asker. Buy yourself some time. Count to ten before saying yes. Try this: "Let me

If a request catches you off guard, don't say anything until you count to 10.

think about it. I have some other commitments that may interfere.''

Losing sight of your own priorities may be the biggest single cause of always saying yes. Say yes to yourself first. Establish clear priorities for the things *you* are responsible for, and keep them in plain sight. Then, when you are asked, you can make a responsible decision based on your own goals—and point them out to the asker if necessary.

Sometimes, even with careful thought, you find yourself saying yes and later realizing that was a mistake. Without delay, get in touch with the person you said yes to, and say something like this:

''Jeff, I have to apologize to you. I forgot all about a commitment I made to the boss, and there's just no way I can do them both. I'm awfully sorry.'' If the situation warrants, offer an alternative: ''I wonder if you've thought about. . . .''

Four Steps to Saying No

If you, like most of us, hesitate to say no because you fear that you will offend someone, memorize this four-step technique:

1. *Listen.* Make sure you fully understand what is being asked of you.

2. *Say no.* If your decision is no, say so politely but firmly. Don't build false hopes with wishy-washy answers.
3. *Give reasons.* If appropriate, explain your reasons; this reinforces your credibility.
4. *Offer alternatives.* Demonstrate your good faith by suggesting other ways to meet the person's need.

In response to a request you simply cannot handle, there are all kinds of things you can say instead of "yes."

"I'm sorry, other commitments just won't permit me to take on a new project right now."

"You know, on New Year's Day I promised my family I wouldn't take on anything else this year. I've been neglecting them too much."

"Thanks for the compliment, but I'm afraid I'll have to decline. Maybe next year."

A company president wrote me from Seattle: "Thanks for teaching me to say no after twenty years in business. I've just written letters of resignation from the boards of four organizations. In every one, I had held on too long, keeping younger people from taking over and contributing. I was under the illusion that they needed my services, since they kept reelecting me. Now I know they reelected me because they didn't want to hurt my feelings! I thank you and my wife thanks you. We're looking forward to more time with the family, starting now."

Saying No to the Boss

Saying no to requests or unreasonable deadlines from your boss is, of course, a different story. The basic strategy here is to remind him or her of your other projects, point out that they are the boss's priorities you are working on, and ask for help in deciding where the new assignment should fall on the list of priorities.

If you are the boss, and you create a conflict of commitments, encourage your team members to point out the conflict in such situations and to offer alternatives. Let them know you expect clear thinking, not blind acceptance. And if others in the organization make demands on your people, support them as they say no to unreasonable requests; if necessary, teach them how.

Check Yourself

How successful are you at saying no? Rank yourself on the following; then do it again three months from now.

Almost never	=	0
Sometimes	=	1
Half the time	=	2
Usually	=	3
Almost always	=	4

Points

1. When I am asked to do something unreasonable or perform a task that someone else should do, I am able to say no without offending. _____
2. I encourage my team members to respond to my unreasonable requests by pointing out how they will interfere with more important tasks and to suggest reasonable alternatives. _____
3. I remain alert to others' requests of my team members and I support my team members when they say no to such requests. _____
4. I recognize that saying no to interruptions is difficult and I practice the many alternatives to saying yes automatically when someone asks if I have "a minute." _____
5. When I say yes without thinking and recognize I've made a mistake, I immediately move to correct the error by telling the person that I made a mistake and the reasons why the answer has to be no. _____

Total _____

Procrastination

Some years ago my family lived in a small New York town called Chappaqua, in Westchester County. Many of the townspeople worked in nearby New York City, and the local train station was a busy place each morning as clumps of sleepy commuters crowded the platform waiting for the train into the city.

One morning, as I sat in the last car chatting with the conductor, he broke off to look out the window. "Uh-oh," he said, "here comes another one." Following his glance, I saw a latecomer rushing down the platform, briefcase in one hand and newspaper in the other, his look of panic increasing as the train pulled away. He was a good 100 feet away, but I could see him seem to make up his mind to go for it, and he began running full out. In a minute or so he had reached the back end of the last car, but the train was accelerating faster as he was tiring, and he realized it was a lost cause. Pulling up with a look of exasperation, he shouted out his frustration to the departing train.

The conductor, who had moved to the door to watch the attempt, shook his head and said quietly, "Mister, you should have started sooner."

If you start on time, you don't have to make a desperate, possibly dangerous, last-ditch effort at the end.

Yet so many of us have a hard time getting started. Postponing that which we know we should do creates numerous problems—for ourselves, our co-workers, and our organizations. But what can be done about it? As is true of so many time wasters that are rooted in the foibles of human nature, the first step is to understand why we do it.

What is behind this phenomenon of procrastination? Often, fear of failure. If the task is risky, if others have high expectations of your performance, if you're uncertain of your skills, you will likely find it tough to start the work, easy to postpone it. Oddly enough, sometimes fear of success can be equally debilitating.

Another common problem is lack of interest in the work. When people have too little to do that is challenging, they quickly sink into boredom. Lethargy, like a fast-growing weed sending out roots in all directions, strangles motivation, and soon people find it impossible to start even simple tasks.

Occasionally people delay work because of feelings of anger and hostility toward someone—usually the person who gave them the assignment, but perhaps the amorphous "they" who run things. They consider it inappropriate to express hostility directly, so they subconsciously choose to get even by sabotaging the work.

Of course we don't want to admit any of these real reasons, so we make excuses: "I don't have all the materials/I have to wait for a report from the other department/I have too many other commitments/I'm just not in the mood right now/There's no rush; it's not due for a while anyway/The timing isn't right/I'll get to it as soon as I clear out these other things/I'll do it later; I work better under pressure anyway."

One of those "reasons" may actually be valid. There are times when it makes sense to put off doing something because the timing isn't right. Thoughtful people know the difference between making an appropriate decision to delay action, and procrastination, which is irrational delay, postponing action without justification. Recognize the other "reasons" for what they are: rationalizations.

The Danger of Delay

Procrastinators are late for meetings and poorly prepared when they do arrive, put off answering correspondence, and don't return telephone calls. They never have their portion of the project ready on schedule, and they don't come up with the information that others are counting on.

They may even be relaxed, easy-going people who don't let things bother them, but in fact they create great stress for themselves with their last-minute efforts. Of course the stress they put on other members of their team is sometimes worse.

Equally serious is the danger of mistakes in the frantic atmosphere of a last-ditch effort. When you put off the task until the last minute, you will almost always produce an inferior job because you have left no time to correct whatever goes wrong—and something inevitably will.

This is why the rationalization "I work best under pressure" is particularly destructive. With the false belief that the work will be better (or at least good enough), people make a conscious choice to procrastinate—thus guaranteeing not a "better" job but its exact opposite.

The tendency to do the things we like, rather than the things we ought to do, is almost universal. Thus if a task is unpleasant, or risky, or frightening, or boring, we are sorely tempted to put it off—even if it is something we could dispense with fairly quickly. Reprimanding an employee, rehearsing that speech, calling the prospect who has turned you down twice already, contacting the client who is rumored to be dissatisfied, writing the unhappy customer—the more we don't want to do something, the farther down in the day we push it.

For most of us, this means that we are tackling our toughest jobs when our energy is lowest. Take a look at Figure 10 and think back to your ideal day (see Chapter Three). Do you honestly think you can do a better job when your energy is down like this? The potential for mistakes under these circumstances is awesome. This is the real reason procrastination is a time waster: If we do something when we're tired, we take longer to do a job, make more errors, and then need still more time to correct them.

The first graph shows our energy level declining during a typical day. If we postpone our top priorities until the end of the day (see "task demands" line), we will have to face them when our energy is largely depleted, thus ensuring poor performance.

Figure 10. Matching tasks to energy level.

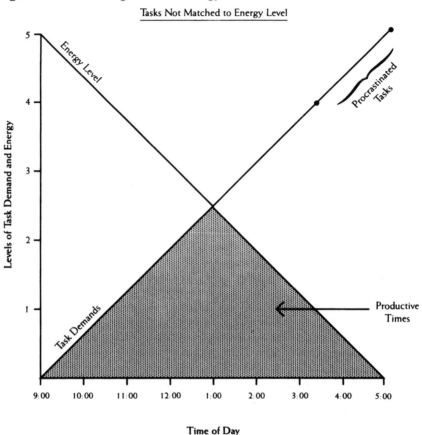

Tasks Not Matched to Energy Level

Note: Low-value tasks matched with high-energy levels, and high-value tasks matched with low-energy levels, produce minimum results.

By targeting our top priority first, we may nearly double our productivity as shown by the second graph.

Curing the Procrastination Blues

The first step toward getting rid of procrastination is to realize that you are in control and make a commitment to yourself to change. Recognize that you have, for whatever reason, devel-

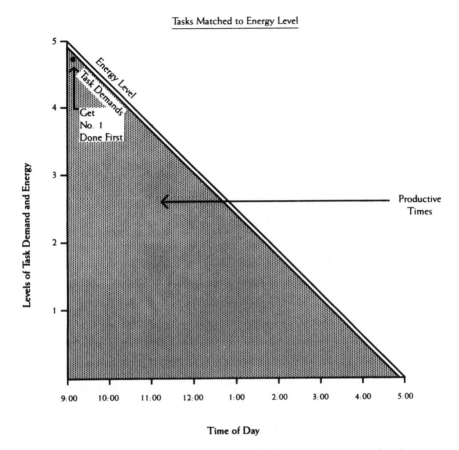

Tasks Matched to Energy Level

Note: The shaded area indicates that times of high productivity are significantly increased when tasks are matched to energy levels.

oped the habit of putting things off, and remind yourself that you are capable of replacing that bad habit with a better one. (Review the three steps to building new habits, Part Three.) Procrastination is within you; it's something you do to yourself. You *can* change it, and you will. Make a conscious effort to develop a "do it now" attitude.

Set deadlines for yourself. Nothing creates a sense of urgency like a deadline. If the project is big, break it down into smaller units; set a deadline for each one. Set a deadline for *starting* the first one. Tell someone what your deadline is; encourage him or her to ask you about it later. Reward yourself when each stage is completed. Try to maintain a focus on the end result. Develop a clear mental image of the finished product, and of how you will feel when everything is done.

When You're the Boss

If people on your team have trouble with procrastination, you can help in several ways. Neil Fiore, in *The Now Habit*, identifies four steps that will help you deal with procrastinators.[1]

1. *Build confidence by fostering commitment, not compliance.* Allowing others to participate in the decisions that affect them increases their commitment. Instead of saying, "You have to have it in by noon," say, "Considering what you know about our schedule, when do you think you could have this part done?"

2. *Focus on starting rather than finishing things.* The idea of being held accountable for doing a big job with a faraway deadline makes procrastinators anxious; they feel overwhelmed by the immensity of the task. Reduce the fear by focusing on the starting point. Instead of saying, "Remember, the deadline is only two months away," say, "When can you get started on a rough outline?"

3. *Give criticism constructively.* Angry, negative criticism is always destructive, but it is especially bad on procrastinators. Fearing for their survival, they lose whatever ability they had to focus on priorities of work. Don't say, "This report totally misses the point." Instead say, "This is a good start. I think if we can add a couple of thoughts on *A* and *B* and strengthen the conclusion, we'll have a winner." Let team members know you recognize their worth as people, and reward progress along the way.

4. *Be decisive and set priorities.* Managers' tendencies to shift priorities as new problems arise are legendary. They are also very damaging to team members and their productivity. Some will be tempted to say, "Let's just wait a day or so and see if they change their minds again." Shift priorities only for confirmed emergencies. Change assignments only if other priorities are

also considered, and alternate the team members you choose for the crisis situation.

"But I work better under pressure. . . ." As a manager, at some point you will have to deal with a team member who puts off an important task with the rationalization of "I work best under pressure." Let's watch how Kay, a fine manager, handles this very common problem. Kay has asked for a meeting with Doug, who has been given a significant assignment but has delayed getting started. Kay is uneasy, and has expressed this to Doug. Doug replies:

"Yeah, I know I probably should have gotten started before now, but I've had all this other work to do. I don't think you should worry, though, because I'm one of those people who works best under pressure. I know I can get to it by Friday. That's your deadline, isn't it?"

"Friday is the deadline, yes. And I'm concerned about your schedule. Are you sure you're not procrastinating on this so you can do other things you'd rather be working on?"

"Oh no, it's not procrastination. I really have had a lot of other work. I planned to start this project later on this week, and I know it will be okay, because I can get a lot of good work done when I'm under pressure."

"You sound convinced about this, all right. But I'm not so sure. Can you explain to me why you think putting off this job until so close to the deadline will help you do a *better* job?"

"Well, um . . . I guess I don't know the *reasons,* exactly. I just know that in the past, when I've been up against a tight deadline, I did a good job. It sorta stimulates me to do my best."

"I know that you believe that, but, frankly, you haven't persuaded me. It's your natural ability to do a good job under almost any circumstances that enables you to perform well under pressure. I'll bet without the pressure you could do even more outstanding work. So here's what I'm going to do. I'm going to ask you to make this your top priority, and I'm going to move your deadline up two days, to Wednesday. And I'll tell you why.

"First, by procrastinating until so near the deadline you aren't allowing any time for planning, and for projects like this, good planning is critical. Second, you're going to want to go over your plan with the others who're involved, and you'll need time for that. Third, you're not allowing time to review everything and make changes if, at the last minute, you discover something that has been overlooked.

"Now, if you think of something that would change my mind, come in and see me at eight in the morning. Otherwise I'll assume you're accepting the new deadline."

Check Yourself

How successful are you at managing procrastination? Rank yourself on the following; then do it again three months from now.

Almost never	=	0
Sometimes	=	1
Half the time	=	2
Usually	=	3
Almost always	=	4

Points

1. When tempted to put off tasks I set deadlines for myself, including a starting time. _____
2. I watch for procrastination in my team, and help them overcome it. _____
3. When facing difficult problems of procrastination, I "go public" by announcing my deadline and asking others to remind me if I ignore it. _____
4. I practice self-rewards when progressing toward a deadline. _____
5. When fear of being wrong influences me to put off decisions or actions, I remind myself of the benefits of timely actions (more time to take corrective action if wrong—and advantage of a fast decision if right). _____

Total _____

Note

1. Neil Fiore, *The Now Habit* (Los Angeles: Jeremy P. Tarcher, Inc., 1989). Copyright © 1989 by Neil Fiore, Ph.D.

Meetings

11

No time waster has had more written or said about it, or more jokes made about it, than meetings. Today no headquarters building would be built without a conference room; some will have dozens. No chief executive of even a medium-size corporation would be without a boardroom; no hotel would be without conference facilities.

What do those who spend time in meeting facilities, boardrooms, and conference rooms say about meetings? That there are too many, with the wrong people, and are poorly run; that they last too long; and that nothing gets followed up. The average manager spends ten hours a week in meetings, and 90 percent of managers say that half of their meeting time is wasted. That's 5 hours a week, 250 hours a year *for each person in the meeting.* In some meeting-prone fields like education, the total is much higher.

The solution to this waste? Have only the meetings that are necessary, and run them tighter.

When You're Running the Meeting

When you're in charge, use the ideas here to keep things moving efficiently. Even when you're not in charge, look for ways to gently incorporate these techniques:

• Decide whether a meeting is really necessary. The amount of time spent—wasted—in meetings that never should have been called is truly astounding. This is true the world over. Australians and Germans, Canadians and Venezuelans, Americans and South Africans—all vote the same: "Have fewer meetings!"

In general terms, there are four reasons for holding a meeting:

1. To coordinate action or exchange information
2. To motivate a team
3. To discuss problems on a regular basis (as in a staff meeting)
4. To make a decision

The last reason is usually suspect. Ask yourself whether your real goal in calling the meeting is to get others to share the risk of making a decision that properly belongs on your plate. Everyone is vulnerable to this at some point; it involves such human characteristics as self-image, self-confidence, and tolerance of risk. It often happens this way: You realize that your regular staff meeting is coming up in a day or two, and so you decide to add the issue as an agenda item "for discussion." You'll get everyone's opinion—maybe, and at considerable time cost—but in the end you'll still have to decide.

Do you really need a meeting? Could you accomplish the same thing with a memo or phone call to all participants? Are you holding the meeting out of habit, rather than need? Could you get by with a staff meeting every other week instead of once a week? Is it time to phase your committee out of existence, now that its work has been completed?

• Prepare an agenda, with time limits for each topic, and circulate it in advance. That way each participant has an opportunity to prepare ahead of time. If a specific amount of time is allotted for each item, you will find it much easier to keep the discussion moving and to end the meeting on time.

• Invite the right people for the right time and the right place. Have present those people needed to solve the problem—no more, no less. Make sure the timing is right. Don't meet too soon, before all the necessary information is at hand; don't delay until it is too late for the outcome to be effective. If the discussion will be lengthy or complex, consider holding the meeting at an outside location.

• Start on time. If you hold up the meeting for latecomers, you reward them and penalize those who made the effort to arrive promptly. Once they realize you're not serious about the starting time, they won't bother to be so prompt next time. And don't backtrack for late arrivals. If the problem is confined to one or two individuals, here's your answer: Put their pet issues at the top of the agenda, and dispense with them first. You probably won't have to do it a second time.

• Dismiss participants after they are no longer needed. As far as possible, organize the agenda around people involved in the topics. Release people as soon as their topics have been dealt with. This is a significant time-saving device which everyone appreciates.

• Stick to the agenda. You have established time limits for each item; once the allotted time is up, move on to the next item. Once people realize you are serious about this, the discussions will become much more focused. If, in spite of your efforts, someone introduces a topic that is not on the agenda, try this:

"That's an interesting point, Charlie, but I'm afraid it would take us into an area that is not on the agenda, and most of us are not prepared for it. How about if we schedule it number one on the agenda for next week, so we can be better prepared and really do it justice?"

If Charlie insists on discussing the matter now, then say, "Okay, Charlie; we certainly want to be democratic about these questions. Let's put it to a vote. How many of us feel as Charlie does that this needs to be discussed right now?"

You can be pretty sure of the results of the vote, because the others know that a detour will lengthen the meeting unnecessarily.

• To stay on track with the agenda, keep socializing to a minimum; permit interruptions from outside only in a genuine emergency. If discussion on a difficult topic becomes stalemated, with one faction trying to force acceptance of its position on another, move to the next item—or adjourn if it's a one-topic meeting. Reconvene the next morning, and you'll be surprised how quickly the matter can be resolved once everyone has gained a bit of perspective.

• Decide next steps. As the last point for each item on the agenda, agree on the next action to be taken—who, how, when.

• End on time. People need to know that the meeting will end when you say it will so they can plan for the time following. If the meeting drags into their next appointments, they will become very resentful; this is a downhill road for any meeting leader. The time-limited agenda will be a big help here.

• Prepare and circulate minutes. Thorough followup depends on good records of what action steps were decided. Minutes will be particularly valuable to those who were unable to attend the meeting.

Admiral Hyman Rickover was famous for running tight meetings. He developed a wonderfully concise format that served as both agenda and minutes. At the beginning of the meeting topics were listed by name with a starting time. By the end of the meeting, the decision on each one had been recorded—yes, no, or hold—responsibility assigned to a particular person, and a deadline established. Rickover would scrawl on a big *R* at the bottom, cross out the word "Agenda" and write in "Minutes," and order copies distributed immediately to those with a right to know.

Agenda/Minutes, Rickover Style

Time	Item	Decision	Responsibility	Deadline
10:00	A	Y	BJ	9/15
10:20	B	N	—	—
10:35	C	H	—	—
10:45	D	N	—	—
10:55	E	Y	CB	10/1
11:00	Adjourn			

How to Get Out of Meetings

We have all had the experience of feeling stuck in a meeting at which we were not really needed. Granted, sometimes this is unavoidable. But sometimes we don't make enough effort to find out the true purpose of the meeting in advance. We could then apply one of the following strategies:

- Go for just the portion of the meeting that relates to you, especially if your boss has called the meeting. Present your argument in terms of the benefit to him: By skipping part of the meeting, you'll have more time to spend on the main priorities that he wants by tomorrow morning. If the meeting has been called by another manager, depending on his or her level, you may need your boss's support for this attempt.

- Use your boss as an excuse. Suppose someone from another department stops you in the hall and asks that you "drop by" the committee meeting tomorrow; it's not clear to you what your function would be. Try to get more information and at the same time build a basis for declining: "I think I might have a conflict with my boss tomorrow afternoon. If you don't mind, would it be okay if I clear this with her before giving you an answer? Now, just to make sure I understand, tell me again—what will you be discussing?"

- Decide things without a meeting. If someone calls and asks to get together to discuss something, ask, "Can't we just do it now on the phone?" Or if a meeting-happy person stops you in the hall and suggests a meeting, say, "Well, here we are together right now; why don't we just decide?"

Similarly, if you suspect that your boss is calling a meeting for the purpose of sharing the risk, say to him or her—assuming you have a good relationship—"You know, whatever you decide is okay with us. Why don't you just decide? Whichever way you want to go, we'll support you."

- Send a written statement as a substitute. Let's say you have been asked to attend a meeting called by another manager, but you think your participation is marginal. The meeting chair is too important to risk offending, but you've got your own work to do. Assuming your boss understands and supports what you're doing, try this approach.

First, phone the assistant of the person who called the meeting: "Sarah, I just got this memo from Harold about the meeting on Thursday and I think I may have a problem with some projects that I'm working on for my boss. It's not really clear to me what would be expected of me in this meeting. Could you help me? What does Harold want me to talk about?"

If Sarah knows, she'll say, "He wants you there for the discussion on *A* and *B*." Now you have to think fast.

"Sarah, if I can't make it, suppose I just give you a written statement on both of those things—which is really all I would say if I were at the meeting—and authorize you to give it to Harold. And that way I can stay out of trouble with my boss."

If Sarah does not know why you're being invited and has to ask Harold, he may come on the line (or he may call you later), demanding, "What do you mean you can't make it to the meeting!"

"Well, Harold," you then say, "you know Tom [*big hint*] is involved in two big projects for the vice-president right now, and I'm the key person in our department on both of them. You've called your meeting for tomorrow, which is pretty short notice for me, and so I asked Sarah if there was any way I could possibly provide you with whatever I can that would be helpful to you, and still not get in trouble with Tom."

Few managers would deny such a reasonable request.

- Hold a phone conference using the three-way calling feature. For more than three people, use speaker phones or phone conferencing arranged by the telephone operator.
- If the budget permits, use video conferencing or fiber-optics conferencing. Sometimes the savings in time and money spent on travel make electronic meetings a more efficient, more economical option.
- Hold a conference by computer, with a chairperson running the meeting.
- Forget the computer meeting and use e-mail instead.

How to Start a Meeting When You're Not in Charge

Often the biggest problem with meetings is that they don't get started on time. Not only does this waste precious minutes at the beginning, it seems to set a lazy, meandering tone for the entire meeting. If you're running the meeting, do not permit any delay. But what if you're not? There's plenty you can do.

Let's consider an example where the person who called the meeting arrives on time, but doesn't start right away. People are standing around in groups, chatting; or simply waiting, tapping their pencils. You can take control. Say, loudly and with a note of surprise in your voice, "Hey, it's ten o'clock." Everyone will stop and check their watches; the chair, who is probably chatting with someone up front, will say, "Okay, let's get started here"; and everyone will silently add, "Amen."

If the person who called the meeting is the one who is late, don't wait. You can say something like this: "Janice is probably tied up on the phone. Why don't we get started, and when she gets here we can just fill her in. This first item, now—what do we all think about this?"

Then, when Janice arrives, summarize: "We could tell you had been held up, so we've gone ahead and discussed the Carson proposal. We took a vote, and it's ten to two against it, if that helps you." And then sit down.

If the meeting chair is known as an ineffective manager, don't try this; you'll create problems for yourself. But a good manager will approve wholeheartedly.

Check Yourself

How successful are you at managing meetings? Rank yourself on the following; then do it again three months from now.

Almost never	= 0
Sometimes	= 1
Half the time	= 2
Usually	= 3
Almost always	= 4

Points

1. I don't call a meeting, and I resist attending others' meetings in which the purpose is unclear. _____

Points

2. My meetings have agendas that are time-limited (time limit set on each topic). _____

3. My meetings start and end on time. _____

4. Participants not required for the entire meeting are encouraged to attend only the part applicable to them. _____

5. When topics come up that aren't on the agenda, I suggest putting them on the agenda for the next meeting so everyone can be prepared. _____

Total _____

12 Paperwork

The age of automation, which was supposed to free American business from the burden of paperwork under which it had so long struggled, has instead only made things worse. Computers don't create less paperwork; what they do is make it possible to create more and better looking paperwork faster and more efficiently. Now that every office has fax capability in addition to computers, the mountain of paperwork is getting taller at a much faster rate.

And what a mountain it is! A few years back one division of a large corporation we were working with removed ten tons of paper during a clean-up campaign. A California personnel company surveyed over 900 personnel directors about the portion of their jobs that was committed to routine paperwork. More than half of them said they spend between one and three hours each day, which works out to as much as roughly ninety-four work days a year. I can think of some fields in which the paperwork total would be far higher. Copies of reports and memoranda are circulated widely, with no one questioning whether they are needed. Top management is bombarded with documents from several levels down, and lower-level managers find themselves submerged in cascades of paperwork from above, which seems to gather authority and urgency at each successive level. The possibility of "computer crashes" dictates that files be backed up on disks as well as on "hard" paper copies so now we have disk files to manage, but we have not gotten rid of our paper files. I can't count the number of people I know who have vowed to put all the vital paper information into their computers and then still kept all the paper files as well as back-up disks.

What do we do with all this paper? We push it around for a while, move it from one stack to another, leave it in the in-basket for a few days (hoping it will disappear, maybe), and eventually file it—where it will probably never be looked at again. Less than 5 percent of filed documents are ever referred to after the first year, but we store them for years, "just in case."

The solution? Devise ways to screen it more effectively, to handle faster the papers that do get through to you, and review skeptically the ones you are accustomed to creating. Be willing to try some unconventional techniques: Stop sending a report to see if anyone misses it! Set up systems and stick to them. Purchase large wastebaskets and investigate possibilities for recycling.

Coming In

Letters and Memos

I've heard it said that William Randolph Hearst never answered his mail; he claimed that after two weeks people either came to see him, called on the phone, or wrote a second letter—and then he would wait another two weeks on that one. I also know of one chief executive of a Fortune 500 corporation who uses what he calls "the ninety-day drawer." All his mail goes into that drawer to "ripen"; he says it is surprising how little of it has any importance after ninety days.

I don't especially recommend either technique, but there are certainly ways we could be handling our mail much more efficiently than we now do.

• Have incoming mail screened. This is far and away the best way to reduce your load. Authorize your assistant to open, sort, and screen incoming mail, using a four-step screening process.

1. *Handle.* As much as possible, encourage your assistant to answer routine mail. Give him authority to discard when appropriate.
2. *Delegate.* If mail coming to you can be answered more appropriately by someone else in your department, your assistant should route it to that person. If it is critical that you know about the situation, he will summarize it for you.
3. *File.* If the matter is not urgent but is something you would eventually want to read, your assistant will place the material in a review file.
4. *Expedite.* This leaves only those papers that require your personal attention. Work out a routine with your assistant: He will mark the key passages and place everything in your color-coded correspondence folder.

• Once you look at it, handle it. If you don't have an assistant to screen your mail, help yourself out by making a decision about each piece of mail as soon as you read it. Throw it out, file it for review later, send it to someone else, or respond to it.

Reports

Look for the summary that all good reports should have (see the following section on producing reports) or have your assistant read and summarize for you.

Be firm; don't waste time on marginally useful material. A few years ago I was visiting the offices of the managing director of a very large consulting company based in Europe. The company has dozens of branch offices and hundreds of associated companies and individuals; the number of projects at any one time can be staggering. In fact, his side table was loaded with computer printouts several inches thick, detailing all the organization's current activities.

"Do you actually read all that?" I asked him.

"Heavens no. Most of it I don't need to, it's just a repeat of last week's report. I wish our system could be set up to give me just what has changed, but until it does . . . do you notice those reports are sitting right over the wastebasket? That's where they will end up."

Journals

Keeping up with the literature in your field can easily seem a losing battle. Almost every manager I talk to admits to a feeling of always being behind in important reading. Here are some ideas:

• Have your assistant skim publications and highlight or summarize key points for you; or assign certain publications to different staff members.

• Subscribe to a digest service. Subscribe to an on-line data bank specializing in your fields of interest. In this way, you can delegate some of the electronic "keeping up" in your field and reduce time wasted in vague, sometimes aimless, electronic browsing.

• Circulate journals among staff people, with a routing slip that has your name at the bottom. Encourage them to make marginal notes of interest items. If a magazine comes back to you with very few notes, you'll know your team members found it of little interest. Consider dropping this subscription.

• Learn to read faster, either through a formal speed-reading course or by practicing on your own. With even a short course in speed reading, most people can double their reading rate with no loss in comprehension.

• The best practice I've encountered was that of a manager who simply checked the articles of interest in the tables of contents and circled or wrote the subject under which it should be filed. If he ever needed it, it could be instantly retrieved. Until then, he wasted no time in reading it or in shuffling it around on his desk.

Going Out

Letters and Memos

Most people spend far too much time crafting their responses to letters or creating their memos. Try these tips for getting the job done faster:

- Consider alternatives. Maybe you don't have to write the memo at all; perhaps a phone call would be better. Same with responding to a letter or memo. A telephone call or e-mail is less formal, friendlier, and faster, usually.

- Delegate writing tasks whenever you can. If your assistant or someone on your staff can do it, let him.

- Make it short. Too many of us are stuck in the nineteenth century style of business writing, leading to cumbersome, lengthy letters with stilted phrases and lifeless clichés. Try writing your letters in a conversational style, say what you have to say, and be done with it. If you can answer the letter or memo in a few words, write your response on the bottom of the original and send it back.

- Make it adequate, not perfect. If your creation is clear and to the point, that's good enough; another hour polishing may not produce a significant improvement. For letters and memos, eliminate first drafts.

- Dictate your correspondence, handwriting is a waste of two people's time. Batch all your dictation together and do it all at once; you can do five letters at one time much faster than you can do one letter at five different times.

- For recurring situations, build a file of "sample" letters; you or your assistant can quickly make minor changes as required for individual responses. Keep these templates easily accessible in your computer.

Reports

- For all reports you are responsible for, develop a standard format to be followed each time. You save time that would otherwise be spent inventing the wheel; you also save your readers' time, for they learn which section of the report will always contain the material they need.

• Make a determined effort to reduce the number of reports you create, and to make each one shorter. Long reports and documents are often not read anyway, at least not in their entirety. By eliminating unnecessary reports at the point of inception, you conserve an enormous amount of time and storage space. From time to time review regular reports to see if people are actually reading them. Test this by preparing one, as proposed above, but not sending it out; see if anyone complains about not receiving it.

• If you are in a position to do so, establish a full set of procedures designed to streamline internal reports for the department or the company as a whole. If you're not in such a position, suggest the idea to the person who is.

Followup System

A good followup system saves you time in more ways than one. You don't have to look far when you need something, because you always know where it is; but you can put it out of your mind until the action is needed.

One is the popular "31-day followup" system. File folders numbered 1 to 31 are used to hold documents until the day they are needed. If you answer a letter on, say, January 18 and want to check that a certain promised action did occur by January 22, put the copy of your response in the "22" folder. If a certain document will be needed for a meeting that is scheduled for February 3, put it in "3." Each morning, check that day's folder as part of your planning routine. Once the followup is complete, the material is filed away in the appropriate subject file, if needed, or discarded if not. Meanwhile, the paperwork is off your desk yet automatically retrieved when due.

Another system uses just six folders. They are labeled Today, This Week, Next Week, Mid-Range (one to three months), Long Range (three to twelve months), and Pending. In each folder go the files, correspondence, notes, and all other papers according to when they will be needed. In "Today," for instance, you would put all the background material relating to projects that are on your daily plan for today. At the end of the day, remove tomorrow's documents from the "This Week" file. At the end of the week, "This Week" should be empty; on Monday morning, material stored in "Next Week" gets moved forward. The file marked Pending is for items for which no date is yet known; when the timing does become clear, put it in the appropriate file.

Both these systems are especially appropriate for those who do not have an assistant. The last one is particularly easy to administer.

If you use an electronic organizer, insert the promised action and deadline while you are talking with the other person on the phone. Tell them you are doing so. Your organizer will then beep you with an on-screen prompt at whatever minute, hour, day and year you have entered. Do *not* take notes and *then* try to enter the information after the phone call. You won't get it done and you will lose your notes.

Storing It When You're Finished: Filing

Establishing a fail-safe system for filing documents to make retrieval possible is best done by an effective manager/assistant team. If you don't have an assistant or if you share support staff with others, be especially vigilant in these basic rules:

- Set up a clear system to designate that a document is ready to be filed: Your initials and today's date at the top is one good way. Set up a separate "file" box or folder for completed work.

- It is your job to designate the name or subject under which the paper is to be filed. Underscore the appropriate word in the document, or write the name on top and underscore it.

- You are also responsible for noting how long the item should be stored. Use this coding, or develop your own:

M		=	destroy after one month
Y		=	retain for current calendar year
Y + 1		=	retain current year plus one
Y + 7		=	retain current year plus seven
UC		=	retain until project complete
P		=	permanent files

You may also need to change your way of thinking about files; many of us are in the habit of keeping papers automatically, without a clear purpose. That quickly leads to multiplying file cabinets.

A manager in London told me a lesson he had learned about paper control ten years earlier. He had run out of filing space, and had put in a routine request for another filing cabinet. The request was refused. When he went to see his boss to ask about it, he was told, "The reason I turned down your request for another file cabinet is that I see no evidence that you are attempting to control the amount of paper you are saving. I'd like you to purge your files by tossing out everything you're not *sure* you will need at some point. Let me know the results, and whether you still need the extra filing space." In the ten years since, he has never needed more than one filing cabinet.

Simplify wherever possible. Have the photocopy of your response to a letter put on the back of the original; you'll take up half as much room in the file drawer. Don't overload your files with documents of doubtful value, especially if there are other copies available. Take a tip from a bank vice-president who never keeps any paper unless it's an original. "If it's a copy," he explains, "all I need to know is who has the original." He says he's had only one filing cabinet his entire career—impressive testimony from the chief personnel officer of a 5,000-person organization.

Check Yourself

How successful are you at managing paperwork? Rank yourself on the following; then do it again three months from now.

| Almost never | = | 0 |
| Sometimes | = | 1 |

Half the time   = 2
Usually   = 3
Almost always   = 4

Points

1. The flow of paperwork is controlled to eliminate all un-necessary forms, reports, and copies of correspon-dence.   _____
2. Up-to-date filing systems are maintained to optimize speed of retrieval.   _____
3. A schedule for purging files has been established and is maintained.   _____
4. Excessive policies, procedures, and other forms of red tape are not tolerated.   _____
5. I have studied and practice speed reading.   _____

Total   _____

Leaving Tasks Unfinished

The art of leaving tasks unfinished takes many forms. When we allow an interruption of any sort, we are automatically abandoning the task we were working on. When we interrupt ourselves—by daydreaming, taking a break, or turning our attention to something else on our desk—we are leaving one thing to take up another. Others suffer, too. In organizations, unfinished tasks take a serious toll on co-workers who are depending on their completion. For self-employed people, unfinished tasks snowball, tumbling on top of each other until they form an avalanche, as each client rightfully assumes his or her project to be most pressing and most important.

Dr. John Mee, former professor of management at the University of Indiana's School of Business, is the only person I know who has studied seriously "the art of finishing." "The gift of the finisher," he says, "is the compulsion to closure." Finishers have the ability to stick with one project until it is completed—occasionally against all odds. Finishers do not tolerate interruptions, except for emergencies. Even then, they resist leaving the current task unless it is absolutely clear that (a) the priority of the crisis is higher than the task being worked on, and (b) their assistance is crucial to solving the crisis.

"Unfinishers," in contrast, are unable, for any number of psychological reasons, to complete tasks. You can recognize them by the trail of partially complete projects behind them. Some may be subconsciously resisting finishing something for fear the work will not be good enough; others are unable to weigh conflicting priorities and so shift from one job to another all day long.

There are always reasons for leaving a job in the middle—sometimes even good reasons. The trick is to exercise the self-discipline to return to it once interrupted, and to leave it in good condition to be picked up again easily.

If you are interrupted in mid-project for a legitimate reason, take the time to prepare. You should be thinking to yourself, I may not see this again for an hour, or even a day. Say to your interrupter, "It will take me a minute or two, but I'll be right with you." Then do whatever is necessary—finish the sentence, complete that column of figures, wrap up the phone call. Write yourself a note describing how you plan to finish the project when you get back, and set it in the middle of your desk with your coffee cup on top.

You have probably already recognized that the problem of leaving tasks unfinished is connected to several other time wasters: lack of self-discipline, inability to set priorities, interruptions of all kinds, personal disorganization. In these connections lie solutions to the art of finishing. In particular:

- Reward yourself when you finish the job—and not before.

- Set deadlines for yourself, but make sure they are realistic. As most of the people interviewed for this book said, experience is a great help in setting realistic deadlines. So learn from your experience. Upon the completion of each project, increase its rewards and its value by writing down what you learned from that project, including what you learned about setting deadlines on that kind of project. The next time you are preparing a proposal to do that kind of project, get out your previous postmortems and review them. If there is no room for a realistic deadline, given your other projects, turn this project down. Otherwise, you will risk leaving all your tasks unfinished. This is a critical time management lesson for the growing segment (almost one-third) of the workforce who are now self-employed.

Most of them will learn it the hard way. If you are one of the smart ones and really want to get your money's worth from this book, learn it now.

• Once you have learned to set realistic deadlines, build in a cushion for those delays and emergencies that you know will arise. This is especially necessary if you report to multiple clients rather than to one manager.

• Keep a clear focus on your priorities. If you are in doubt, confirm them with your boss. The boss's priorities should be your priorities.

• Learn to anticipate problems and prepare for the unexpected delays.

• Keep your desk clear; don't let visible evidence of one unfinished task nag you into interrupting another.

Check Yourself

How successful are you at completing tasks? Rank yourself on the following; then do it again three months from now.

Almost never	=	0
Sometimes	=	1
Half the time	=	2
Usually	=	3
Almost always	=	4

Points

1. When interrupted in the middle of a task, I make every effort to postpone or suggest alternatives to the interruption so that I can complete the task I'm on.   _____

2. When it's not possible to postpone or eliminate an interruption, I take steps to leave the task in the hands of someone who can complete it or in a state where I can pick it up with minimum delay after the interruption has ended.   _____

3. Since a cluttered desk provides constant interruptions, I practice keeping my desk clear except for the task I'm working on.   _____

Points

4. I take steps to control noise and visual distractions in my work environment. _____

5. I have a plan for screening telephone calls, drop-in visitors, and paperwork, and I practice it. _____

Total _____

14
Inadequate Staff

The question of inadequate staff has two aspects: inadequate in the sense of not having enough people, and inadequate in the sense of lack of skills. Both are fixable.

Too Few People

In today's competitive environment, restructuring, downsizing, and cutback management are common. Smart managers have to learn to accomplish more—or at least the same amount—with fewer people.

Teach Better Time Use

The most direct approach to the problem of understaffing is to help people learn good time management techniques. We already know that anyone who makes even a halfway serious effort can save an hour a day; two hours a day is more common for those who are committed to gaining control of their use of time.

With good coaching, you can lead your team members toward success. Show them how to block interruptions—

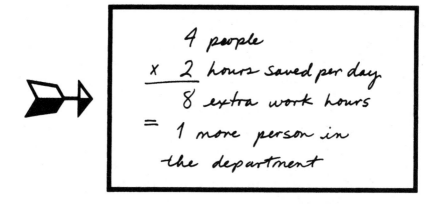

including interruptions from you. Demonstrate the art of setting goals for the day, and putting them in priority order. Let it be known that a desk piled high with files does not impress you. The trick, I think, is to let them know you are engaged in the same learning process yourself. If staffers resist the idea of keeping a time log, for example, tell them you are doing it, and describe how you have benefited.

Staffing Proposals

The first step in any understaffing situation should always be to see what improvements can be made with the current team. Assuming you have done that and it isn't enough, you will have to develop a proposal to higher management for additional positions.

Prepare a thorough cost-benefit analysis, outlining what can be achieved by new workers. Time logs are essential to this process. With them, you will be able to demonstrate which tasks now being done by team members could be done by lower-scale employees. The logs will also help you chart new projects that could be accomplished with the freed-up time.

Inadequate Skills

The presence of a team member who does not have the skills to do the job means one of two things: An error was made in the hiring process, or training for the particular position was not what it should have been.

When it is apparent that you have the wrong person in a job, it is an injustice not to take action. First, you must consider the interests of the individual. He or she has a right to know about unsatisfactory performance. In many such cases, people assume they have been doing all right, since nothing was said. Second, the manager has the right to a competent team. Finally, the organization has the right to expect that every position will be filled with qualified people. Don't delay facing the issue of inadequate personnel; harm is done in all quarters.

The question of poor training is something else again. Responsibility for seeing that people are well trained rests with their managers. The department manager, usually with the assistance of the human resources unit, conducts a needs assessment survey, develops a training schedule of both external classes and on-the-job special coaching, and establishes a system to evaluate the various training modes and follow up on results. That's the ideal. In the real world, all too often training is scattered, haphazard, uncoordinated—if available at all—and usually the employees have to request it.

You may or may not be in a position to influence the shape of the training in your organization, but you can exert an enormous influence on individuals on your team by the way you guide and lead them through their day-to-day work.

For the self-employed person, many of the points made under Time Topic 6, Ineffective Delegation, also apply here. If you don't have the staff you need:

- Form temporary alliances
- Form partnerships on a project-by-project basis
- Trade services
- Give interns valuable professional experience
- Out source
- Hire part-time help
- Hire full-time staff
- Streamline your business goals

Check Yourself

How successful are you at managing your staff? Rank yourself on the following; then do it again three months from now.

$$
\begin{array}{lcl}
\text{Almost never} & = & 0 \\
\text{Sometimes} & = & 1 \\
\text{Half the time} & = & 2 \\
\text{Usually} & = & 3 \\
\text{Almost always} & = & 4 \\
\end{array}
$$

Points

1. In filling positions I ensure compliance with all approved steps in the hiring process including reference checks, skillful interviewing, and so on. _____
2. In filling staff positions I ensure that a job description exists for the position, determine the skills required to perform the tasks described, and rate the candidates' qualifications against these job requirements. _____
3. Where requisite skills are lacking, I recommend appropriate training based on needs assessment. _____
4. I ensure effective followup after training to determine the extent to which desired behavior changes have occurred. _____
5. In situations of apparent understaffing, I check first to determine how effectively personnel are being used. _____
6. To cost-justify additional staff, I require time log analyses to determine what additional staff would do, at what cost, and what those helped would do with the time freed up. _____

Total _____

15
Socializing

In Time Topics 2 and 5, you learned many techniques for controlling interruptions from phone calls and drop-in visitors. Both have appropriate social ingredients, and both also have the potential to shift over into inappropriate socializing. But the presumption in both those earlier sections was that the original motivating force was business. Someone in your department stops by to ask you a question; someone else calls for some information. The focus here is purely social: A friend calls or, more likely, wanders in to your office to chat or—let's call it what it is—to gossip.

The causes of excess socializing are not difficult to spot: Loneliness. Need to change pace or scenery. Gregarious instinct. Curiosity. Desire to be informed. Ego. Fear of offending. Inability to say no to socializers. Inability to terminate a conversation with a "talker." Poor physical location that encourages visiting. Assuming the good-will ambassador role to all passersby. An excuse to avoid dull work.

It is true, of course, that the workplace is a primary environment of social contact and that developing friendships with our co-workers is one of the most satisfying aspects of our job. It is true that good personal relationships are necessary for effective teamwork. It is true that the ability to get along with others is a commonly requested job qualification. It is true that in certain fields a friendly, outgoing approach is absolutely vital to success.

But this is also true: It is easy to overdo it. Test yourself: Take a time log for just two days, in which you concentrate only on socializing. I think you'll be astounded when you see how much the total time adds up to, and if I'm right, you'll want to make some changes. Here are a few ideas:

• *Have visitors and phone calls screened.* If you have an assistant, give her the authority to screen all calls and all visitors; this will go a long way toward reducing the incidence of purely social contacts. It is then up to you to keep the focus on business when the calls and visitors are put through.

• *Evaluate your physical setup.* If everyone passes your desk on the way to the coffee room, you can be sure you'll get more than your share of visitors. If you can, have your office moved. If you can't, at least keep the door closed for periods of concentrated work. If you don't have a door, move your desk so it's facing away from the main traffic flow. If you can't do that, at least don't feel you have to stop work and greet every passerby; train yourself not to make eye contact. Find a hideaway.

Don't keep extra chairs in your office. Or your personal coffee maker with several cups. Or a candy jar. All these signal, "Come in and sit a while."

• *Develop techniques to cue the end of social time.* If someone is in your office ostensibly for the purpose of work but wants to chat a while, you need to take charge. Allow the social portion of the visit for as long as you consider appropriate, then signal nonverbally that it's time to get to work. Shift from the relaxed way you were sitting to a more upright, ready-for-business position. Open up your folder, and say, "Now, I think what we need to talk about for a few minutes here is. . . ." Or, "Thanks for letting me know about that vacation spot; sometime I'd like to hear more. But right now I need to ask you about. . . ."

If you're part of a group standing around visiting—the proverbial water-cooler gossip scenario—and you believe it's time to disengage, say something like this: "Well, I guess it's back to work for us poor peons. I've got a real doozy of a deadline; see you guys later." And leave. It's friendly, nonthreatening, and odds are someone else will respond, "Hey, speaking of work . . ." and the group will disband.

Some people have the knack of leaving a group discussion silently but without offending. They smile, nod, shrug their shoulders as if to say "Boy, I wouldn't know what to do in that situation either," and simply turn and walk away.

• *Stand up.* If you see a habitual gossiper approaching your office, head him or her off at the pass. Stand up, walk around your desk to greet the visitor, shake hands, and say this: "Hey, Pat, good to see you. What's up?" Take a step toward the door. "I was just on my way down to accounting to check on something. Tell you what: Walk with me and we can talk for a few minutes on the way."

• *Don't give in to persistent talkers; keep your focus.* If your attempts to switch the conversation to business topics don't get through—and with some people they won't—hold your ground. Suppose you open up your folder and ask the first business question and your visitor says, "No, wait a second, I gotta ask you something: Did you hear what happened to Clarence?"

"Well," you say, "yes I did, and I was surprised, and I would like to go into that with you some other time. But unfortunately I just can't right now, because I'm looking at a really tough deadline for my boss. Could we talk about it after work? Let's see now, how about Step B? That's where we have the conflict with last year's numbers."

Your written daily plan is your ally here. As you mention your deadline, point to the plan. If your visitor is persistent enough to ask, "What kind of deadline is it?" you can turn your plan sheet around and show it: "Here it is, item number 2, 11:30. I have to have this on my boss's desk by then."

• *Put visitors to work.* For those drop-ins who blithely ignore your efforts to return to work, one man developed this truly ingenious technique. He kept a folder in his drawer marked "Visitors," and in it he put chores to give to those who wouldn't go away—the more boring the task, the better. "I have a couple of minutes of work to finish up here," he would say, "before we can talk. Hey, by the way, while you're sitting there, would you

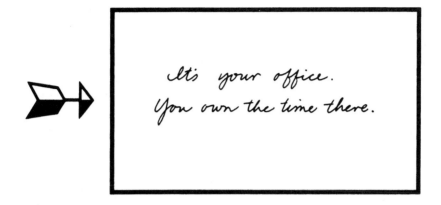

It's your office.
You own the time there.

mind adding up this column of figures for me? By the time you're finished I should be done here, and then we can talk." He said his buddies soon stopped coming around.

• *Learn how to deal with the boss.* All well and good, you say, but what if the person who sinks down in the chair for a social chat is my boss? First of all, make sure you *look* busy. Through all your visual, nonverbal cues, make it appear that you are working and that stopping to chat is just that—stopping work. Much depends on your boss's personality and the rapport you have together. Your main strategy is to show that limiting the socializing is in the boss's own best interest: "Could we maybe continue this later? I really need to continue on this project I'm doing for you." Put just a tiny bit of emphasis on those last two words.

If you are in the boss's office and the conversation drifts too far into social waters, say something like this: "I'd better get back to work or you won't have your report in time for the meeting." Or, "If you don't mind, I have some things for you on my desk that I really should get to."

For the self-employed and for the organizationally employed in certain professions, networking, marketing, and socializing tend to blur. Since you never know ahead of time where that next contact or next valuable piece of information or next project or next full-time job—if that's what you're looking for—will come from, it's very difficult to know when networking, marketing, and socializing have gone overboard. As with predicting, setting realistic deadlines, planning, and crisis prevention, managing networking, marketing, and socializing is a skill you can get better at with *experience.* Just as you set aside time to plan before and to evaluate after the completion of projects, so setting aside time to evaluate your networking, marketing, and socializing can yield more productive results.

Check Yourself

How successful are you at controlling socializing? Rank yourself on the following; then do it again three months from now.

> Almost never   = 0
> Sometimes   = 1
> Half the time   = 2
> Usually   = 3
> Almost always   = 4

Points

1. I keep my door closed to discourage socializing, while making sure anyone on business knows it's open to them.   _____
2. I practice the techniques for terminating conversations without offending.   _____
3. I avoid socializing situations, except when appropriate, by having calls and visitors screened professionally.   _____
4. I ensure that location and position of desks are planned to minimize socializing.   _____

                                             Total   _____

Confused Responsibility or Authority

Two people each think they're supposed to do a task—so it gets done twice.

Two people each think the other person is supposed to do a task—so it doesn't get done at all.

One person has been given a task, but the other person doesn't know it and so doesn't cooperate.

Two people each think they have been given the authority to do something, and they give conflicting instructions to others.

When there is confusion about who is responsible for what, or a mismatch between responsibility and authority, much time and effort are wasted.

Responsibility Issues

Questions about confused responsibility center around job descriptions. When job descriptions are poor—or nonexistent—opportunities for confused effort are rampant. If your job description is vague, or if you do not have one, you do not have to continue in this inefficient mode. Take charge of your own job. Draft a list of responsibilities, or a full job description, for your manager's approval. If there is an overlap with another employee, real or imagined, identify areas of duplication and sit down with your manager to try to resolve them.

In many work settings, inappropriate usurpation of responsibility by others presents a real problem to conscientious workers. On the face of it this might appear to be a blessing: Someone is taking over work that you should be doing. But it is a mistake to permit this to happen, for one simple reason: You are responsible for the results, and being held accountable for what someone else does puts you in an impossible position. If you find yourself in this situation, go to the other person and talk it over candidly. Take your job description along, and say something like this:

"You know, I think we have a problem here. It looks to me like you're working on some things that I really should be doing. I don't think we need to bother the boss over this; I'm sure we can work it out. As I read over my job description, those two items fall under it, so it seems to me I should be doing them. Maybe we should check your job description; maybe there's a mistake and this area of responsibility is on both."

You may get this sort of response: "I don't think you need to worry about it. All the boss really cares about it is that it gets done, not who does it; so why don't I just keep going?"

Your answer: "As long as it's in my job description, I'm accountable. If you make a mistake, *I'm* responsible." And that should take care of the problem.

If the other person sincerely protests that he's supposed to be doing the task, then you must bring the question to your boss for clarification. Probably one of two things will happen. The boss will say, "It was an oversight; I'll take care of it." Or: "I'm probably responsible for this mix-up; I did assign that project to Doug. Never occurred to me that it really belongs in your bailiwick. You're right, but I don't want to take it away from him in the middle. Let this one go, and let Doug be responsible for the results. We'll straighten it out next time around." In either case, make it a point to follow up with the boss—tactfully, of course.

Authority Issues

Responsibilities—questions of who has the *duty* to do what tasks—are usually laid out in job descriptions, and therein lies the main avenue for resolving such problems. Authority is a different kettle of fish. Authority is the *power* to do the tasks you are responsible for. Power to sign purchase orders for necessary supplies. Power to collect information from other departments. Power to use the time and talents of other team members.

Grievous mistakes are made every day by managers giving people the responsibility for a job without also giving them commensurate authority to get the job done. As they struggle conscientiously to do the work, blocked at every turn, an incredible amount of time is lost. Not to mention the damage to the morale of a loyal worker.

Mary liked her job very much; Dennis, her boss, entrusted her with a good deal of responsibility, and she was given more challenging tasks than any of the other assistants in the unit. Still, she felt uneasy with her new assignment. The boss had just returned from a time management seminar and told her to start screening his calls and visitors. When she asked how he wanted it done, he replied, "Just find out what they want. If you can't get the answer for them, make an appointment or set up a call-back for me." And then he walked into his office and closed the door—something he rarely did.

A short time later, Lew, one of the experienced team members, came to see the boss. As Lew approached Dennis's door, Mary tried to intercept him. "Can I help you, Lew?"

"Nope," he answered, "just need a minute with Dennis." And in he went, leaving Mary feeling as though she had failed.

Who's at fault here? Not Mary; she tried to do what had been asked of her. Not Lew; he had no way of knowing the new procedure. The fault is with Dennis. He should have explained to his team what he was trying to accomplish with the screening, and asked them to cooperate with Mary.

Problems of confused responsibility and authority are especially likely to surface when two organizations combine, as is common today with mergers and acquisitions. I watched an especially time-wasteful situation unfold in a merger situation recently.

A small manufacturing company, Company A, was bought out by much larger Company B. The former owner of A was designated general manager of the combined organization, Company A/B, and designated his old office manager as his assistant. The president of Company B, now CEO of Company A/B, asked the new assistant general manager (former office manager A) to collect some confidential personnel files from the person who had been office manager of Company B—a person, incidentally, who had expected to be named assistant general manager. Office manager B refused to turn over the files, even though office manager A pointed out the request came from the president. Office manager A then asked for the name of B's manager, hoping to clear the logjam, but that turned out to be a vice-president who was out of the country for several weeks. The CEO was also unavailable just then, so office manager A had no recourse except to return to his office empty-handed.

How many people lost time here? Office manager A, who was unable to fulfill his assignment. Office manager B, who used up time protecting his turf but in the end had to give in. General manager A/B, who had to be interrupted so the problem could be explained. President A/B, who also had to listen to the problem and step in. Plus all those involved in untangling strained relations. And all this could have been avoided if the CEO of Company A/B had taken a moment to call office manager B and alert him.

Giving authority to someone entails making sure that others are made aware. To be effective, authority has to be made public.

Check Yourself

How successful are you at clarifying responsibility or authority? Rank yourself on the following; then do it again three months from now.

Almost never	=	0
Sometimes	=	1
Half the time	=	2
Usually	=	3
Almost always	=	4

Points

1. I regularly update job descriptions of all people for whom I am responsible to ensure that their exact responsibilities and authority are clearly defined.   _____

Points

2. When delegating responsibility, I ensure that commensurate authority is also delegated. _____

3. When checking the causes of inadequate delegation, I automatically check the possibility of a lack of commensurate authority. _____

4. In cases of confused responsibility and authority, I automatically check the possibility of overlapping job descriptions. _____

Total _____

Poor Communication

Get a group of businesspeople together, ask them to tell you about the biggest foul-up they ever heard of, and nine times out of ten it's a story about miscommunication. The punch line usually goes like this: "When we finally figured out what was going on, this poor guy says, 'But I thought you said. . . .'"

Some people communicate effectively without trying. Others try without communicating. It's a critical skill that is not well understood. Too often we take it for granted. We know how to talk, others know how to listen, and that's all it takes, right? Wrong. Effective communication is infinitely more complex than that.

Everyone involved in a communication must infer the same meanings from the words that are used; a misunderstanding on even one word can cause havoc. The communicator must take care to choose the channel that best fits the situation; the recipient of the communication must be in the right frame of mind to receive the information; the timing must be right for both parties. The communicator must take care to give enough information that the recipient fully understands, but not so much that the recipient tunes out. Communication is not simple, but it is the medium in which work gets accomplished, and so it behooves us all to learn better techniques.

Steps to Better Communication

No matter whether you are talking informally with one person, addressing a familiar group, as in a staff meeting, making a phone call, writing a memo or letter, or giving a formal speech to a large gathering, the process of effective communication has certain basic steps.

1. Clarify your purpose. If you're not sure why you are about to communicate something, your uncertainty will likely reveal itself and hamper the effectiveness of your communication.
2. Select the appropriate channel. Should you write a letter? Make a phone call? Go talk to the individual in person?
3. Compose the message for maximum clarity. Use simple language; your goal is to be understood, not to show off your vocabulary.
4. Transmit as clearly as possible (how's your diction?), with the least possible interference, and at the time when the recipient is most receptive.
5. Request feedback to check understanding.
6. Never *assume* you are on the same wavelength as the person you are working with, in regard to the goals of a project. *Ask.* Find out before you travel many miles down the road toward a goal that is not wanted.

Being a Good Listener

Some years ago I came across this piece of information: The average adult is only 25 percent effective in listening. We spend more time listening to others than speaking, reading, or writing, yet we are taught very little about it. Dr. Ralph Nichols, former professor of communications at the University of Iowa and University of Minnesota, has done seminal work on the subject of listening, and today there are many books, articles, and seminars based largely on his research. If you are concerned about your own communication skills, you'll want to consider these ideas adapted from Nichols's work.

1. Ignore your prejudices. Listen with an open mind; do not prejudge.
2. Avoid overstimulation. Don't overreact to emotionally charged words.
3. Listen for important points. Ignore trivia. Get key facts that relate to main points.
4. Take notes to reinforce understanding and avoid storing excess information in your brain.
5. Avoid distractions. Concentrate.
6. Ask questions.
7. Detect and interpret body language: gestures, facial expressions, tone of voice.
8. Read between the lines. What was *not* said?
9. Avoid the temptation to interrupt.

Using the Right Words

The most amazing things can happen in interpersonal communication because two people understand one word in their own very different ways. Each thinks the other ascribes the same meaning to it, and so neither even considers the possibility of miscommunication.

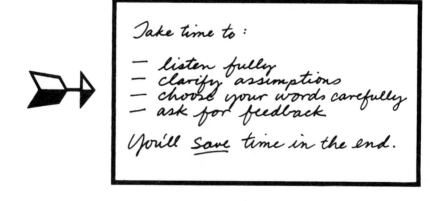

Take time to:

— listen fully
— clarify assumptions
— choose your words carefully
— ask for feedback

You'll <u>save</u> time in the end.

In the business world, it often happens like this: The boss dictates a quick memo to the staff, instructing that something be done, then leaves on a trip. After the boss has gone, the assistant types up the memo and distributes it. Before long one of the team members comes by and says, "What does this sentence right here mean? If you look at it one way, she wants one thing, but it could also mean this. Which is it?" The assistant, who had not considered the second interpretation, now realizes that indeed it isn't clear. But the boss is not available, and so everything freezes until she can ask her about it.

To prevent such time-wasting situations, the boss should get in the habit of briefing, or backgrounding, the assistant. If the boss had preceded the actual dictation with a background remark—"I want everybody to draft some ideas on how we can improve the space planning around here"—the assistant would have been able to clarify even ambiguous phrasing because she would have known the boss's intent.

Other problems surround common phrases to which certain people ascribe special meaning. Sometimes we have to learn the hard way. A draftsperson in an engineering firm was instructed to do something "as soon as possible." The project manager used the phrase as a code for "this is urgent." The draftsperson understood it to mean "when you can get around to it."

The next time, the draftsperson was prepared with a constructive suggestion: "You know, the last time someone asked me to do something 'as soon as possible' I got in trouble because I didn't understand exactly what he meant. It would help me a lot if we could set an actual deadline for this."

Understanding Nonverbal Communication

Communications experts tell us that as much as 70 percent of all communication is nonverbal. By the set of our mouth, the expression in our eyes, the way we sit in our chair, we say as least as much as we do with the actual words we say aloud. More, usually: We can control our choice of words, but we cannot always control these nonverbal responses; they "speak" the truth.

For example, what does it mean when someone sits with arms crossed, legs extended out straight and crossed at the ankles, and body facing away from you, with only the face turned in your direction? It means the person has stopped listening to you.

When You Don't Understand

For communication of all kinds, skillful use of feedback will prevent misunderstanding. If you are the communicator, learn the fundamentals of feedback. If you are the receiver of the communication, insist on it.

This is a common complaint: "The boss says it real fast and hopes I guess the rest." A manager who tosses out instructions and then dashes off, not courteous enough—or smart enough—to take the extra few minutes to ensure understanding, creates nothing but chaos and wasted time. Let's imagine the scene.

The boss is leaving for a three-day trip, and has called in Steven, a new project manager, for a last-minute review. Speaking rapidly, he ticks off four or five items he expects Steven to follow up on while he's gone, then asks impatiently, "Got it?"

Steven, uncertainty written all over his face, says, "Um . . . yeah, I think so." The boss, oblivious to all the cues that clearly announce Steven does *not* understand, snaps, "Okay, that's it then. Ask Karen to come in, will you?" And repeats his performance with his assistant.

Here's what Steven should do. Even though he is reluctant to admit his uncertainty, even though the boss is impatient and gruff, he should say simply, "No, I don't understand." Temporary discomfort is much better than wasting three days of work on misunderstood directions.

And what should Karen do? Take a tip from Shirley Wilson, the wonderful assistant who taught me about personal organization (see Time Topic 12). I did to her what I have just told you not to do: stood over her desk and rattled off a number of instructions, grabbed my briefcase, and dashed out the door. It was not until I was getting into my car that I realized she was right behind me. Calmly, completely composed, she got into the passenger seat and quietly said, "Now, why don't you go over it all again, and I'll make complete notes this time. You drive, and I'll write. I'll drive your car back from the airport, and come pick you up when you get back." And she pulled out her notepad. I never did that to her again.

Check Yourself

How successful are you at communicating? Rank yourself on the following; then do it again three months from now.

Almost never	=	0
Sometimes	=	1
Half the time	=	2
Usually	=	3
Almost always	=	4

Points

1. I clarify the purpose of any communication before attempting it. _____
2. I compose the message to ensure that it cannot be misunderstood. _____
3. I select the channel (verbal, written, nonverbal) carefully before communicating. _____
4. I choose the timing of communication to ensure maximum attentiveness. _____
5. I check feedback to ensure that the communication was understood as intended. _____

Total _____

Inadequate Controls and Progress Reports

We have already discussed the benefits of setting deadlines on tasks, of dividing large projects into smaller segments and setting interim checkpoint dates, and building in a cushion to allow for the inevitable delays (see Time Topics 1, 3, 8, and 10)—and the terrible tangles that occur when we fail to do those things. In this section we focus on a key step in this process, a step so vital—and so often overlooked—that it has earned a place of its own on the list of worldwide time wasters.

The need for control is essential in any large project, and the most useful medium of control is periodic progress reports. Whether the project is one you yourself are managing or one you have delegated to others, the flow of events must be organized so that you can maintain forward momentum, evaluate performance against the plan at any point, and spot problems promptly.

An excellent system for monitoring projects is the timeline, which some have called the way to eliminate half of all crises. A timeline has three essential ingredients, depicted graphically in Figure 11: a deadline, a target, to provide a cushion—at least 20 percent, and checkpoints for regular progress reports.

The purpose of progress reports is to provide a structure by which you can spot deviations, potential problems, or other unexpected occurrences that may have a negative effect on the

Figure 11. Project timeline.

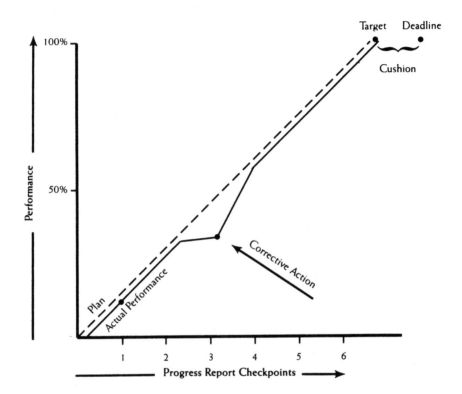

Project Timeline

project—and spot them in time to take corrective action while it can still be done cost effectively. The timing of the interval between reports will depend a great deal on the nature of the project and the final deadline; you might need progress reports quarterly, monthly, weekly, or daily, although monthly and weekly are the most commonly used.

These reports serve another function, too: Each one becomes a deadline in itself, encouraging and goading you to complete a portion of the project by a certain time because someone is expecting a progress report—even if the someone is you. These checkpoints foster a sense of priority and provide an automatic device with which to measure your progress.

For any major project you are responsible for, I recommend

that you draw up a project plan sheet that outlines all the action steps needed, correlated to due dates. Do a separate sheet for each project. Once you have established the final deadline, the "cushion" target, and the checkpoints, transfer all those dates to your monthly and weekly plans (see Time Topic 3). The priority of the project will be reflected in the priority assigned to each checkpoint date in your daily plan.

Progress Reports in Action

Let's take a look at how the process works, starting with one of your own projects. Assume that the head of your department wants to create a new training program for new employees, and you have been assigned responsibility for a training video on time management for support staff team members. You would start by considering alternatives and investigating relative costs. Then, once an approach has been agreed upon, you would think through all the steps necessary to develop the video according to that approach, and all the substeps, and put them into a reasonable time frame, taking into account the final deadline you have been given. Your Project Plan Sheet might look something like Figure 12.

Now let's look at a project that you have delegated to someone on your team. That person will be responsible for developing the plan for the project, but you should be aware of the general outline of the plan, and should have checkpoint dates on your own calendar.

It's best if the person who will be performing the project suggests the timetable. When you assign the project, ask, "How should we go about this? When would you feel comfortable reporting back to me on your progress?"

"Well, it's a three-month job, how about once a week, on Fridays, then every day in the last week?"

"That sounds okay to me, if we can make one change. Since this is our first big project together, how about daily the last two weeks?"

Progress reports are meaningless if they are too late, so if

Figure 12. Sample project plan sheet.

Training Video	Month Jan					Month Feb				Month Mar				Month April				
	1	8	15	22	29	5	12	19	26	5	12	19	26	2	9	16	23	30
1. Check alternatives	S	F																
premade? Do it here?																		
consultant?																		
2. Prelim. budget	S	F																
3. Choose format			F															
4. Content outline			S															
— check other shows			/															
— ideas from staff			/															
— first draft						/												
— final draft								F										
5. Script								S										
— first draft											/							
— final draft												/						
6. Visuals										S								
— interview prod.co's											/							
— sign contract												/						
— story boards												S	F					

S — Planned date to start
/ — Dates to check progress
F — Deadline date to finish
X — on target
Ⓘ — Behind target

a progress report is missed, be sure to check with your team member.

"What happened?"

"To tell you the truth, I didn't have much to report but I knew something would be cleared up by Monday, so I decided to wait till then."

"Well, that's not the way I like to do things. I believe it's much better to say on the agreed day, 'Nothing to report; update coming Monday.' So let's let this be the last time, okay?"

If it happens again, call the person in a second time and say, "Looks like we'll have to have daily progress reports for the rest of this week."

The president of a New England college developed a Control Matrix (see Figure 13). Each of his senior team members used the form to schedule key action steps on current projects; both the president and the department manager retained copies. They met on the scheduled report days and both noted the status of each project on their copy of the matrix.

Use whatever format works best for you; you may prefer to devise a custom-made project plan sheet that reflects your own field. The format is only a tool with which to capture a useful idea: periodic progress reports that will tell you when you're in trouble, in time for you to get out of it.

Check Yourself

How successful are you at maintaining control through progress reports? Rank yourself on the following; then do it again three months from now.

Almost never	=	0
Sometimes	=	1
Half the time	=	2
Usually	=	3
Almost always	=	4

Points

1. I establish deadlines on all important tasks.   _____
2. I require regular progress reports on all important tasks.   _____

Points

Figure 13. Sample control matrix.

Department _Development_

Project/Date	Action	Action	Action	Action
1. On-Campus Executive luncheon 1/20	Plan: *Finalize program* 1/27 Action: *Program settled* 1/27	P: /*invite guests* 1/31 A: *Roster complete* 1/31	P: *luncheon* 2/6 A: ✓	P: A:
2. Estate Planning Project 1/27	P: *Attend Seminar and report* A: 2/9 *Seminar Evaluated*	P: *Prepare direct mail program* A: 2/23 *Approved*	P: *Initial mailing* 2/27 A: *Delay in mail room*	P: *Reschedule mailing* 3/3 A:
3. Alumni Telethon 1/27	P: *Prepare timetable* 2/3 A: *Approved*	P: *Recruitment of volunteers by* 2/17 A: *Completed* 2/17	P: *Training Seminar* 12/24 A: ✓	P: *Telethon* 3/3-7 A: ✓
4. Parents Fund Appeal Letter 1/27	P: *Draft approved* 1/27 A: *OK* ✓	P: *Mail* 2/3 A: ✓	P: A:	P: A:
5.	P: A:	P: A:	P: A:	P: A:

Points

3. I require performance standards on important, repetitive tasks.   _____

4. I ensure that controls are set on routine procedures to alert appropriate people to any serious deviation of performance from plan.

Total   _____

Incomplete Information

All of us have known the frustration of being stalled by missing information. The material we need to incorporate into our project is late, and when it does finally arrive, it's only half of what we asked the other party for.

The mistake here? Assumptions. We assume the other party knows what we need, and why. We assume the other party sees the request with the same urgency we do. And we assume that, since the information must come from someone else, there is nothing we can do—our hands are tied until it arrives. Wrong on all counts.

Work Out a System

The best way to guarantee you'll have the information you need when you need it is to organize your needs systematically. Think through the entire project, asking yourself these questions:

- What information will be needed, at all stages of the project?
- Where will the information come from? What departments, which individuals are involved?

- Who will be responsible for gathering material? Assign responsibility for collecting the information; on a very big project, spread the responsibility among several team members.
- Work out a schedule, and backtime your request: When will you need the information? How long will it take the others to produce it? When should you make your request?
- What might go wrong? What would be the most likely source of delay? What steps can you take to prevent delays or buffer your project? Are there alternative sources for the information required? (Review the steps of contingency planning in Time Topic 1.)

Requesting Information From Others

Obtaining needed information from others—especially those outside your team—requires tact, diplomacy, and resourcefulness.

Start by making your request in the most appropriate format—phone call, informal note, formal memo or letter—considering the nature of the project and your relationship to the other party. Be direct, straightforward, friendly, and thorough. Describe fully what you need, and when. Unless it is clearly inappropriate, also explain *why* you need the information. This will go far toward developing understanding and empathetic cooperation.

If the information is not provided in a timely way, talk candidly with the person involved. Explain all the reasons why the information is important; it is possible he or she does not understand. Go over again what you need, and strive for agreement on a deadline. If the material is still missing by that agreed-upon time, contact the individual a second time. Reiterate your need and its importance, perhaps more strongly.

And what if that doesn't work either? Go to the other person's office, sit yourself down, and say something like this:

"Charlie, we've got to have a talk about this. I am in serious trouble with my boss over this situation, and I have no intention of staying in trouble. He's a great guy, but it is no fun being around him when he's mad. So here's what I'm going to do. I'm going to go ahead and make up my report, and when I get to that section where your information goes, if I don't have it I'm going to write 'Information withheld by Charlie P.' And then my boss is going to come after you, and I would hate to see you in that spot—there'll be blood all over the floor in here. So let's you and me try to get together on this thing, so we can stay friends. Next Tuesday is the deadline. I'll be looking for your material in my in-box. Thanks for your cooperation."

Along the way, two devices may prove useful in your search for cooperation.

1. *Response deadline.* Within a reasonable time limit, set a deadline for receipt of the material. Send a written confirmation of your request, with all pertinent details; at the top write in large letters RD FRIDAY NOON, indicating unmistakably that the information is required by noon on Friday. If the other party cannot comply, he or she is obligated to advise you promptly and negotiate a reasonable date or suggest an alternative.

2. *Unless-I-hear memo.* If what you are awaiting is a decision, you can prompt a response, or obviate the need for one, with this technique. Make a copy of your original request and clip a note to it like this: "Attached is a copy of my request for your decision on Project X. It is time for me to take action. Unless I hear to the contrary by Friday, August 12, I will assume that you approve of my outline of the project and will proceed accordingly."

Let's close with this gentle reminder: when others ask you for information or a decision, respond promptly. Cooperation is a two-way street.

Check Yourself

How successful are you at managing information flow? Rank yourself on the following; then do it again three months from now.

Almost never	= 0
Sometimes	= 1
Half the time	= 2
Usually	= 3
Almost always	= 4

Points

1. I provide for the acquisition of information needed by myself and my team for decisions, planning, and general information. _____

2. I hold regular meetings with my team to ensure that they are informed. _____

3. When appropriate, I call brief meetings to coordinate work in progress among my team members. _____

4. When necessary information is withheld, I practice making the priority clear to the withholding party, then, if not successful, going up either to my own boss or to the withholding party's boss with a request for assistance. _____

5. I discourage requests for irrelevant information. _____

Total _____

20 Travel

The young professional at the time management seminar had brought along, as instructed, both his time log of three days and his personal list of time wasters. I asked him to show me his time log, and the first day's record:

"Tell me, Stan, what did you achieve during the flight?"

"What do you mean?"

"What did you accomplish during this period with the diagonal line cutting through 9:00 a.m. to 12:15 p.m.?"

"Well, I got to Minneapolis."

Without saying a word, I held up his log, side by side with his time-waster list, and turned both papers around so he could see them. Number one on his time-waster list was "travel." Slowly, as he realized the irony of his situation, a big grin came over his face.

"Guess I could have used that travel time better, huh?"

Stan, like so many others, had to learn to shift his thinking about travel. If you are well organized, travel time is not a time waster, it's a time-*saver*. It's as if the airline, in addition to providing the service of moving you from one city to another, has given you a marvelous gift: uninterrupted work time. There is no phone, no casual visitors, no meetings, and if there is a crisis, someone else takes care of it! In one hour of flight time, you can accomplish what would take you three hours of "normal" time in the office. That's tripling your productivity!

Pretrip Planning

Making travel time work for you, instead of against you, starts while you're still in the office. There is much you can do ahead of time to make the most of your travel time.

Consider All Alternatives

The first thing you must do when the idea of a trip comes up is ask yourself, "Is this really necessary?" Look at all the other ways you might accomplish your mission.

• Invite the other party to come to you. The president of a California organization that had acquired a company in Great Britain lamented to the CEO that, having just returned from a grueling four-day trip to London, he had to turn around the following week and go again. The CEO asked, "Why are you going there? Why not invite them to come here?" A brilliant move: The president saved two days of travel time, and the London officers had an opportunity to meet their American counterparts in a relaxed setting.

Consider asking your client to come to your offices, where you will have all information available at your fingertips, plus the facilities to make a full presentation.

Insurance agents and security reps who practice this say it saves them one to two hours a day in travel time. Further, when appointments are canceled, they are in their offices, where time that would otherwise be lost can be put to productive use immediately.

• Send someone else. A junior associate, attending the meeting as your representative, can have an invaluable learning experience. If the subject area involves someone else's specialty, send the specialist.

• Use other communication forms. Can you accomplish

your purpose with a letter or a phone call? A teleconference or video conference can avoid several people traveling all day for a one-hour discussion.

- Postpone. Don't overreact and go rushing off to solve the problem; wait till you have all the facts. Don't schedule the meeting if a key decision maker is not available. If it isn't urgent, wait till a more convenient time. Suggest, "I'll be out in your area in a week and a half; can it wait till then?"

Coordinated Planning

Once you have determined that the trip is necessary, look for ways to get the most out of your time. Plan the itinerary to get the maximum use of your time from the moment you leave until you return. Wherever possible, try to group appointments together. Are there others you can visit on the same trip? Can discussions of other subjects be consolidated? If you have layovers, put that time to effective use. Schedule appointments at airports, make phone calls, or do some reading.

Carefully plan a take-along list. You cannot make decisions on a project unless you have the necessary background files with you. Be sure to include all the tools you'll need: writing materials, calculator, dictating machine, laptop computer. Don't forget extra batteries and the phone cord for uploading material to your assistant's computer.

Prepare a detailed appointment schedule with names, addresses, and phone number of all business contacts, including home numbers, if possible, in case a change of plans becomes necessary after business hours. Dates, times, and places of appointments should be listed, along with any pertinent instructions on locating the address.

Travel Arrangements

It is folly to make your own travel arrangements; turn the job over to a pro—your assistant, the company travel coordinator, a travel agent. After your appointments are confirmed, hopefully by your assistant, have the flights booked accordingly, not the other way around. If possible, try to avoid arriving or departing during the local rush hour.

Whoever makes the arrangements should give you a flight schedule complete with flight numbers, meal service, departure and arrival times, ground transportation details, and hotel reservations, with address, phone number, and reservation number. Ask for an extra copy to leave with your family.

If you travel frequently, make up a checklist of personal items for both cold- and warm-weather destinations; you don't want to have to take time for a quick trip to the store for something you forgot to pack. Strive wherever possible to restrict your luggage to a carry-on bag; you will save much time on arrival.

Working en Route

If possible, don't drive yourself to the airport; take a taxi or the airport limousine. You'll avoid the parking hassle, and you can have the highway time for reading or catching your breath. Leave the office in plenty of time; if you must make a mad dash to the plane, you'll be tempted to sink back and relax once you sit down, instead of working. Give yourself a cushion; use those few minutes of preboarding time to make phone calls, from the pocket list prepared just for this purpose. Or mentally rehearse your presentation. Or work on your correspondence file, which is right on top in your briefcase. Don't overlook the value of these tidbits of time. Ten minutes may not seem like much, but six ten-minute blocks add up to an hour.

On economy-class flights, ask for an aisle seat. You'll have a bit more room to spread out, and it will be easy to watch the other rows and move to a spot next to an empty seat, which you can use to good advantage as you begin to work. If you're traveling with an associate, don't sit next to that person, unless the two of you need to confer. Be candid; explain that you need quiet time to work.

In your briefcase, you have arranged in folders all the projects you intend to work on during the flight, with the number-one priority item on top. A color-coded system can be very useful here. You may, for example, have a file marked "Correspondence," with nonurgent mail and memos saved expressly for this purpose. For each one, make notes in the margin with instructions of who should handle and how, and slide each completed piece into a colored folder. Once you arrive, ship all completed work back to your assistant (using prestamped envelopes). Call your assistant to alert her to what you are sending, and get an update on events back at the office. If you are using a laptop or portable computer, you'll doubtless be handling urgent as well as nonurgent business. You'll plug your computer into a hotel telephone and unload it into your assistant's computer or a holding station.

Many travelers use this time to catch up on business reading. Or to think—even a short flight may give you the quiet time you need to solve a problem.

During Your Absence

Your team members may think the world of you, but that doesn't mean they aren't happy to see you leave for the airport. It's only human nature to want to slack off a little when the boss is gone. You can circumvent Parkinson's Law (work expands to fill the time available) by asking all your team members this one question before you depart: "What will you have accomplished when I return?" Their responses are both a goal and a commitment, and since they will likely want to impress you, they will set high goals. Discuss possible problems that may arise, and let your team members know the extent of their authority in your absence, which decisions they can make and which should await your approval.

If you'll be gone more than a few days, have your assistant digest your mail, summarizing and highlighting the key points, and forward it to you by fax or computer. If you don't have access to either, jot your notes in the margins and send the items back in prestamped envelopes, with authority to write and sign full responses. You'll return to a beautifully empty in-box.

Make arrangements to phone the office at a set time every day. If any problem arises, your team will know you'll be available sometime that day for questions and guidance.

When You Return

Discipline yourself to deal immediately with the notes from the meeting, the expense reports, the ideas you collected during the trip. If necessary, spend the first day in a "hideaway" location—an empty conference room, someone else's office. If you procrastinate, thinking "I'll just do that tomorrow," you'll very likely end up putting it off not one day but several. By the time you get to it you'll have forgotten some of the details, and the value of the trip itself will be diminished.

Just for Commuters

If you travel to work by train, bus, or automobile, you can put that time to good use. In all the years I rode into the city on a commuter railroad, one hour each way every day, I never ceased to marvel at the numbers of people who spent the time reading the newspaper, playing cards, or dozing. Those who used their commute time productively—for business reading, writing reports, or answering correspondence—were definitely in the minority, often almost nonexistent.

A cellular phone in your car may be a reasonable investment if you spend several hours driving. Even if stuck in a traffic jam, you can be working. On the drive home at the end of the day, phone business contacts on the West Coast—or the reverse: call East Coast colleagues on the way to work if you live in the West. You can also use the time to listen to audiotapes about your field or general business topics. Carry along a small portable dictating machine, and make notes to yourself while traffic is stalled. Even if you ride the subway, a personal tape player will permit you to use the time to good advantage.

Check Yourself

How successful are you at managing travel? Rank yourself on the following; then do it again three months from now.

Almost never	=	0
Sometimes	=	1
Half the time	=	2
Usually	=	3
Almost always	=	4

Points

1. When the possibility of travel arises, I consider the alternatives such as telephoning, a phone conference (in the case of a meeting), writing, inviting the person to come to me. _____
2. In planning my travel, I examine the purpose carefully and list all materials necessary to accomplish the purpose. _____
3. I pack materials for use en route in my briefcase for easy access. _____
4. My itinerary includes all travel destinations, names of key people with phone numbers in case of travel delays, appointment times, locations, and purposes. _____
5. Before leaving, I discuss with my team what each expects to have done by my return. _____

Total _____

Part Three

Using Time to Live and Work Better

Section A
Successful Top Time Managers Reveal Their Biggest Challenges and Their Biggest Secrets

One continuing source of surprise to me is the number of people in all walks of life (including professionals and managers) who are struggling, almost desperately, to manage their time and gain control of their lives. More amazing is the number of people, almost as large, who have become so overwhelmed that they've given up hope of achieving any real order and are simply trying to avoid falling off the treadmill. But most surprising is the third group—that growing number of individuals and organizations who have taken the classic principles of time management, applied them to their own unique circumstances, and created personalized systems that enable them to direct their energies toward professional goals and then enjoy the personal space they have created. These real-life, contemporary examples continue to inspire and educate me, as they raise new time concerns and then offer the philosophies and practical solutions they have developed to make time management work for them. There is hope.

One universal characteristic of these top time managers is that they view the development of their time management systems as an ongoing process and they view themselves as lifelong students of the subject. Here is what they had to say:

Dr. Eleanor Brantley Schwartz, Chancellor of the University of Missouri, Kansas City:

Time management is central in my life. In order for me to be productive with my jam-packed schedule, I need to plan the slots in which each necessary thing will get done and then see that it gets done within that slot.

I have always had a busy life from the time when I was in

school, held a full-time job, and was raising two children as a single parent. This could have been a high-stress situation, so I developed time management techniques out of sheer necessity. I would write from 4 A.M. until 6:45 A.M. when I would wake the children. We always did as much preparation as possible for going to work and going to school the night before. We tried to have everything we needed by the door and lunches prepared the night before and waiting in the refrigerator. Now I have household staff, but they, too, must be managed.

I have always tried to do two things at once, when the tasks permit this. For example, once I got dinner started, I folded clothes as I kept the dinner preparation moving. Or I would write papers in my head, while cleaning up the kitchen and doing dishes. I have always sequenced my errands to make a complete circle from my home and back, to avoid crisscrossing my path and wasting travel time. I also know which items I buy at which stores. I buy all those items when I am at a particular store, and, conversely, I do not need to buy those items *unless* I am at that store.

The most devastating time waster is disorganization. Group like tasks together. Keep your desk in order. Keep your clothes in order. Have a place for everything and everything in its place. Put tools of whatever kind—physical or electronic—right back in their place after using them. This will *consistently* save time that adds up in a big way. Don't put the tool down. Put it away. This applies to filing, also, whether you do the filing or delegate it.

The biggest time-saver is to stay focused on the task you are doing. I keep trying to master this skill. The temptation is great to take a break, even a psychological break in which your mind can wander to something which seems more important or more interesting or more pressing or more troubling. The temptation is great to respond to interruptions, to the telephone, to visitors. The temptation is also great to quickly take a moment—which is never a moment—to get some other task out of the way, to get a sense of accomplishment by getting at least some little task done—instead of focusing your brain power on the challenging, more difficult task at hand.

My greatest time management tool is my team—when I am willing to use it fully. If I am willing to sit down and say, "Help me. Will you take this task?" And to someone else, "Will you take this task?" And to someone else, "Will you take this task?" As chancellor, my team includes four vice chancellors, thirteen deans, and a personal staff of three. To help make it possible for students and faculty to achieve the highest quality academic experience, we must function effectively as a team.

One feeling you must address as a team leader is, "I'm not sure this person will necessarily do the task exactly the way I would do it." And that is true. But sometimes, even often, you find that they do the task in a new, imaginative way—and that it's better.

Also, sometimes there is a crisis. And then you have to accept the task as it is done, or not have it get done at all. However, you do everything you can to ensure that the task is carried out in an adequate way according to acceptable standards.

Develop the habit of discussing the task: its steps, its processes, its deadlines, mutual expectations about the benefits of carrying out the task according to certain standards. This is a skill, a time management skill you can develop: to delegate with the result of building a team, but *without* stifling imaginative thought. Eventually, you and your team members become so good at this process that it becomes streamlined and the resulting greater productivity is achieved with an even lower investment of time in delegation.

Sometimes, inevitably, there is so much that really needs to get done, that it does seem as if there is more than one number-one priority. Sometimes, in responding to other people's agendas, which you must do in a university or other large organization, there develops what does seem to be chaos, stress, and disorganization. You must recognize when this is happening and take time out to regroup. You must reassess the direction you are headed, put yourself back in the direction you want to be going, and then do the tasks that will take you in that direction.

Another benefit of time management for me is personal time. As chancellor, I am required to live on campus. It's part of my job. If I did not apply time management, I would never have any personal time. Time management helps me find some time to myself—and that is a value.

Growing up as the oldest of six children in a large family helped me learn to sort things out quickly and to zero in on what needs to be done.

Phil Gitlen, an attorney in the state of New York:

Making choices is only the first challenge. Then you must *live* with your decisions. That's a real skill. And a necessary one, if you are to go forward without wasting emotional energy that should be focused on implementing the decision you've made. Once you've made the choice, accept the fact that you've also chosen *not* to do or *not* to have all the things that were included in the other choice. That's part of life. Recognizing it frees you to go forward without a lot of baggage that wastes your time, your focus, and your equanimity.

My laptop with its modem is my portable office. I can do legal research from wherever I am. I don't lose ideas as they come to me, because I simply record them in my laptop. After I've researched and conceptualized a case, sometimes it all comes together while I'm on the ski slope. So one time management tool that works for me is to complete the intellectual preparation and then go do something else, while the case jells in the back region of my mind. Sometimes this works better than consciously addressing an issue past the point of productivity. *Letting your mind do the work for you is a way of delegating while you do something else.* So (as I explain to my partner), I'm actually working at the same time that I'm enjoying myself on the ski slopes.

Another time management tool that works for me is to think before I write. That usually means that I don't need to write as much when I do sit down to write, because I know where I'm going. The sorting and sifting of ideas that many people do on paper I do in my head before I start writing. Personalized time management techniques like these are very helpful in professions which require intellectual activity, so that your energy is focused on the *results* the intellectual activity is supposed to achieve. Otherwise, prolonged intellectual activity can be inefficient, can wander, and not be very productive economically.

Experience is also a valuable tool in a profession like mine. Having information in your head is even more efficient than having information at your fingertips so that you can retrieve it through your laptop. Beyond that, real *knowledge*, based on experience, surpasses any information source as a time management aid in quickly identifying issues to be addressed and possible steps to be taken. Nutrition, exercise, recreation, and sleep are also time management necessities for achieving peak performance. No time management tool, including the fastest computer, will ensure optimum achievement if your mind is not functioning and alert.

There is also no question that people function better when they are not under extreme stress. Establishing conditions with enough order so that you can focus on the task instead of on outside pressures and deadlines also frees you to be creative and do your best work. My son recently had several applications due for several different prep schools. Each application required an essay and the deadlines for all the applications were very close together. My son and I discussed the prospect of his trying to write all the essays in one or two nights before the deadlines. We considered the possible effects on the quality and outcome of his applications. Then we planned backward. He set dates to complete each essay. Then he broke each essay into interim goals, such as isolating the main idea and putting it down in writing, doing an outline, writing sections, and completing a first draft. He worked these interim goals into his calendar, around his current school activities.

The payoff came, not only when he received his notice of admission to prep school, but even earlier, when he came into the room one night and said, "I've got my section written for today, so I'm taking the rest of the night off to watch TV." No doubt the remainder of the essay was jelling in some remote corner of his brain, while he spent the rest of the evening enjoying his favorite television show.

Planning backward from the deadline goal, creating nonstressful conditions in which to carry out your best intellectual activity, and then stepping back to let the subject ferment—I've found these steps to be effective time management allies in producing results when the product is not an assembly-line widget, but a creative outcome within professional and intellectual boundaries.

Jim Van Houten, an insurance salesman who is now a top insurance manager:

When my wife and I were first married, I said to her that I would like to make a pact with her regarding my work. I would work three—never more than four—nights a week selling insurance (in addition to my sales work during the day) for five years. On the other one or two weeknights, I would be home and on weekends we would do special things like going to the movies and out to dinner. My goal would be to accumulate enough regular premium payments and enough investments so that I could then cut back to one or two evenings of selling a week. I said to my wife that after seven years I wanted to have accumulated enough regular income and investments so that I would be through working evenings, and we could live very well. And we have done that, and still managed to have a lot of good time to ourselves. One key to this whole plan was having my wife in on the plan from the beginning, understanding it, agreeing to it, and cooperating with it. When I came in contact with the classic principles of time management for achieving demanding goals, the requirement that the goals be owned by those affected and owned by those who would have to cooperate in achieving them leaped off the page and hit me in face. I knew from firsthand experience how important it was.

I have also worked very hard to implement principles of time management in specific ways. "Do nothing you can delegate" is a powerful idea that I have tried to put into practice by training, motivating, empowering, and inspiring the people who work for and with me. There is no better way to permanently rid your life of the unwanted kind of stress than to know that you have helped develop those who work for you into capable, autonomous, reliable people who can handle any situation when you are occupied elsewhere.

Two other very important tips: First, learn speed reading. I've read thousands and thousands of books and articles and my comprehension is still increasing. When you read slowly, your mind gets bored and wanders and you have to go back and re-read the material. Reading a lot also gives you a great knowledge base from which to make effective decisions more efficiently. Second tip, never give out your car phone number to anyone except your spouse, your assistant, and one or two other key people, at the most.

Dr. Leo Corriveau, a superintendent whose New England schools have achieved recognition for innovation and results:

As superintendent of schools, I supervise twelve school sites. Time management is critical to my survival, but I arrived at it by trial and error. My time management system is still eclectic. It's a work in progress. I am never satisfied.

I read about and I observe people who are more successful than I am in achieving goals in complex situations that require management of other professional people. I am always a student of how these people manage. Without time management, none of us could carry out these highly professional jobs.

I have been in the business twenty-five years and I'm forty-seven. I taught eight years and became an administrator at a very early age. When I was a younger administrator, around age thirty-six, I looked at other administrators and I thought, "Wow, these guys are ancient."

But I have learned the value of experience as a highly important tool for time management and for success. There are a lot of shortcuts that can help young administrators coming out.

There are several key ingredients for choosing where to focus your efforts. First, you must have a decision-making model. It has to become a model for your whole life.

Second, you must have a plan to execute your decisions. Ours is a comprehensive quality system. Everything we do is designed for that plan to be successful. It focuses all the energy and the time management of everyone in the system. Third, people must *understand* where we're going. Because time management is about what gets done in a period of time, communication is a vital time management tool. Once we know where we're going, we're more likely to get there. And when our whole school system—administrators, teachers, students, parents— knows where we are going, we are all more likely to get there. So for me managing my *own* time is not enough.

Communicating effectively to and with others is essential for time management throughout the organization and for effective achievement of short-term, long-term, and complex organizational goals that involve educational processes.

What do you do when you can't do it all? What I've done through delegation is to *create leaders*. Delegation has been the thing that has really helped me. People have helped me. I could not do it alone. When you help create other leaders, you have taken a giant step forward in the maturation of your time management process.

What I found in Woodstock (Vermont) High School was that you have to make choices. And you have to prioritize them, based on a lot of factors. I can't repeat enough that a decision-making model is invaluable for helping you make choices. Compare it to budgeting software that won't permit you to leave out important steps. Evaluation is also a crucial part of your decision-making model. You have to keep notes of what you do. You have to go through each part and study the impact on the whole. You must do a lot of data analysis. You can't fly by the seat of your pants anymore. As Edward Deming said, the most important skill for leaders of the twenty-first century is *the ability to predict. To predict, you need a system. And experience.* I would summarize what I am telling you by saying that one of the most critical time management tools is to figure out how you need to be spending your time before you spend it.

In working with students to help them develop their time management skills, we have found that a decision-making model helps them tremendously—and they enjoy using it. When students explicitly identify factors that are part of the decision-making process and then outline the steps necessary to reach effective decisions, they develop greater confidence and skill in making time management choices and life choices. I strongly believe that decision-making skills should be taught long before students reach high school.

I am often faced with two number-one priorities. It happens all the time. I have to work on them both at once. You just have to. I can't always lay one aside while I finish the other completely. Today for example, I have four or five. And I can't prioritize them away. I must take care of them. For example, one complex, ongoing number-one priority is developing the school board agenda, putting together all the items that go into the package, grievance items, renewals, searching for new teachers, planning. Pulling them together is just *one* of my number-one priorities. Then I use Alec's priority grid with the decision-making model to develop and recommend a plan for implementing the decisions of the school board.

In high school, you studied every subject every night. In college, you found out after the first semester that you could juggle—and that you had to juggle, in order to get things done in the proper order to meet deadlines. You didn't simply tackle every subject every night. You had to prioritize.

One big time-saver for me is screening phone calls. My secretaries need to be very competent people. They do a lot of screening of what I call fire drill calls. Effective screening is very helpful. So the people working with me are very important. They also help me keep my desk clean.

I've also given a lot of thought to the question of integrating one's professional and personal life. And you know, I can't. During the week, my life belongs to the school district. My family life is really set aside until Friday evening, and doesn't always materialize then, because often there are school functions on Friday nights.

Jim Lange, a pre-med senior at Iowa State University.

I usually study until one in the morning, sometimes two. My alarm goes off at 6:55 A.M. I get up at 7:10, put in my contacts, drink juice, shower, get dressed, shove the toast down the toaster, put on my shoes, slap a bagel in the microwave, eat the toast while the bagel heats, catch the bus at 7:40, read the newspaper while I eat the bagel on the bus, and go to my eight o'clock class.

At noon, I grab something out of the machine at The Hub and eat lunch on my way to the Soil Tilth Lab, where I have a job from 12:30 to 4 P.M. on Mondays, Wednesdays, and Fridays. From four to five, sometimes I spend an hour on the Internet or talk by e-mail with my girlfriend, who's majoring in biology at another university. Then I catch the bus shortly after five. When the weather's good, I like to run. If it's bad, I try to hit the gym or the rec center.

When I get back to the apartment, I throw in a load of laundry, transfer a few dirty dishes from the sink to the dishwasher, eat something, and settle down to study. Once in a while, we play Nintendo or watch something on TV. Then I study until one or two and go to bed. My roommate and I switched his bed around so the light wouldn't bother him.

On weekends I study or work at my uncle's farm. The farm gives me a break, and I need the money. I was making payments on a Mazda with 130,000 miles on it, and the repair bills were killing me. I got rid of it, and now I'm making payments on a Ford Fiesta that gets forty miles to the gallon. There's nothing between me and the road—but that's why it gets forty miles to the gallon.

Last semester I scheduled two afternoons a week to work with a doctor doing genetic research at a hospital thirty miles away. That semester I worked at the Soil Tilth Lab on weekends. I also tutor freshmen and sophomores.

Every summer I take two weeks to backpack and travel: the Appalachians and east coast, the Rockies and west coast, Arizona and Mexico, or Seattle and Canada. That time to unwind is necessary to me.

I also waste time. The cause of most of my time wasters is procrastination. When I have a project that I fear will be difficult, lengthy, or boring, I waste time to avoid starting it. Now I'm studying for the MCATS (Medical College Admission Tests). I hope to get into the M.D./Ph.D. program. It's an eight-year program in which you graduate with your M.D. and a Ph.D.

The truth is that time management is critical in any student's life. But trying to get your money's worth means that you will always be pushing the limit on what can be squeezed into a *finite* amount of time. So your life may sound stressed, even when you think you are working hard, playing hard, and achieving your goals. My question is, "Do I want to spend *all* of my life like this?" I've already borrowed thousands of dollars to attend college, and I have eight years to go.

Dr. Julia Files, Mayo Clinic, who has been recognized in magazine articles as an extremely effective, highly successful physician:

Time management controls my life. Every day I get up and I try to do it better. I run a minute-by-minute schedule, not an hourly schedule. Every minute and everything in my life is totally scheduled, just by virtue of what I do in my profession.

Over the years, I have become more proactive and better organized with my time. In college it was possible to study the night before the test and do well. Medical school was another story! It required continuous studying and effective management of a lot of information to perform well.

As a working mother of three small children I am now accomplishing more each day than I would have ever thought possible. Small children teach you to approach tasks in increments. It has now become impossible for me to commit to one thing in an "all or nothing" response. I am now forced to do things in small steps as interruptions are the norm.

I have been forced to learn the skill of doing things in small pieces, by learning to focus on that one immediate task without being distracted by everything else that is waiting for me. I find this useful not only in my profession, but also in my home life. For example, I recently gave a talk. I had to start my preparation more than a month in advance. In the past, I would have begun my work one or two nights before, but with my current level of obligation, I know that I can't stop the flow of events to spend an entire evening in concentrated preparation. Therefore, I had to learn not to be worried by the fact that I could only dedicate thirty minutes at any one time to the project. By resolving to get the most out of that thirty minutes, it is possible to work successfully in small focus steps and be prepared to give the speech when the time arrives.

One of my biggest time wasters is the telephone. I know that I can lose a lot of time by talking on the phone, however, I know that I use it as a pressure release valve. It helps me to take a few moments and talk with my friends or my mother in the middle of my day, so I can then return to more focused concentration. I have found that a cellular phone has allowed me to use my time in the car for returning patient phone calls and making appointments. This has afforded me some time savings.

What is the biggest time saver in my life? I don't know. I don't yet use a computer, but I have set aside time to learn computers as they pertain to medicine. I haven't yet been able to do this, although I have signed up for a course.

My personal life is currently very challenging. I have three children, aged four and under, and I work full time. I have found that it is essential to have the appropriate support system in place, as it is impossible for me to do everything. I have a nanny and I have someone to do the housecleaning once a week. Luckily, I have a husband who is very involved with our children and he helps with meal preparation and some of the child care issues that we encounter. It is just as important to delegate tasks to other people at home as it is in the office.

What do I do when I find myself faced with two number-one priorities? I think that this is a very tough question, and I know that when it happens to me I have found that focused concentration on the task at hand is essential. The knowledge that another important task is waiting for you cannot prevent you from carrying out the task at hand. So, I try to create the conditions for focused concentration. I am very good at tuning out external interference, and when I need to, I close the office door, turn off the phone, and/or ask for help. I also find that I can get a lot of good planning done in the car and also in the shower.

In some way, I hope your readers will feel better knowing that they are not alone. I am truly a cliché, a working mother who is trying to juggle too much. I see the effects of the same stresses I encounter on my women patients and truly understand how life in the 1990s can negatively impact health and well-being. I too live with the same pressures and feel that this constant need to balance career and family helps me to be a better physician.

The key time management principles I want to pass on to my children are: Be organized. Make it a habit. Do it every day, as I feel organization is the key to tranquillity. Be a list maker and stay focused on the task. My mother told me something that I always think about. When she was in college, one of her professors told her, "I don't need to see how well you perform on your tests to know what kind of student you are. All I need to do is to go to your dorm room and open up your sock drawer, then I will know what kind of person you are and what kind of student you will be." I know that when my sock drawer is out of control, my life is out of control. It's a good barometer.

Margot Wilson, a realtor based in Arizona who is in the top 1 percent of sales nationwide for her company:

We humans are no more productive than we ever were. We're *less* productive. We're busier. We have a mania about keeping busy. My theory is that keeping busy achieves three goals: (1) it lets us avoid reflection, (2) it lets us skip personal experiences that we might have to recognize as unsatisfying, and (3) it gives us something besides weather to complain about. In Arizona, we need more than weather to complain about. But for those of us who are self-employed, the complaint target can't be our bosses.

I've used computers since my first word processor in 1978, to the tune of hundreds of thousands of dollars in equipment, so I can keep updated and make my world more fun and profitable. You have to be computerized, and you have to keep up on computers. I budget two to three hundred dollars a month for electronic updating. I don't spend that much every month. But the money is there when I need to replace my computer, upgrade, or make other electronic investments.

Computers can be big time wasters, too. I took one computer course. I spent one Fourth of July weekend with a manual and that was it. Now I keep up because I have to, but I also delegate a lot of the learning of electronic technology to my assistant. I hired her partly because she's good at computers and good at mastering the manuals, but she was not always that way. She was a friend of mine. I kept telling her she needed to learn computers and she said, "No way." Ironically, she now works for me, and she knows more about electronic time management than I do.

But the mind is the most powerful time management tool available to us. Much more creative—and efficient—than any computer. We absorb things on so many levels, process them in all kinds of intuitive, intellectual, and emotional ways, then draw them out when we need them, often years later. I'm aware of the literature on mechanical and human parts becoming more alike, more interchangeable, even merging. I may change my mind about how far electronic time management can go, as it gets faster and faster and more and more sophisticated. I'm open to it. In addition to my continuing investment in computers, I use a personal digital organizer. I do not use a laptop because it can fry vital information if left in a car under hundred-degree plus conditions under hot Arizona sun. People who leave laptops in cars in thirty-below-zero weather run the same risk with their important information. You think it won't happen, but it only takes once. In that respect, a paper organizer is superior. As with a laptop, it can get stolen. But it can't freeze or fry.

Also, despite all the back-ups and all the preventive utilities you can run on your computer, it is a machine that will at some point crash—as most software manufacturers warn in the directions included with their products. When that happens, your professional life can be at the mercy of your fallen computer in a big way, and you may be facing a time management problem far greater than falling behind in paper filing. So I use computers. But I recognize them for the time management risks they are. And I haven't even touched on the subject of how much time you can waste wandering around the Internet. Do I need to? In the end, a quick mind is the best time management tool you have. All the electronic aids in the world won't help unless, as you use them, you are smart in applying the real principles of time management.

I enjoy shopping for nice clothes—after all, I've earned

them—and I make the time to shop. I also enjoy movies, going out to dinner, and having interesting friends, male and female. I have a complete office in my Mercedes Benz, I clean my own house because I can do it more quickly and efficiently than someone else can, and I do my own grocery shopping at any hour of the day or night, including the wee hours of the morning.

The best time management advice I can give is to have confidence in yourself. Without hope, there is no action.

So *don't get discouraged.* Reprioritize every night. Then go to bed, relaxed in the idea that by reprioritizing and then sleeping, you are taking the two best steps you can to achieve (1) the application of focused concentration to your projects and (2) long-range sustainability.

Dave DeBord,* *a highly respected landscape architect with twenty-three years experience:*

Honesty with yourself about what you as a professional can realistically achieve in a finite period of time is the most important principle of time- and self-management. Just as the laws of physics will not permit you to cram an unlimited number of objects into a finite physical space, so the laws of time management will not permit you to cram an unlimited number of projects into a finite period of time. Don't tell your client you can get something done in four weeks if it's going to take eight weeks. Don't tell yourself you can do something in an hour if it's going to take two hours. Don't rationalize that you'll be *able* to get something done later, when it needs to be done now. *You* know you won't get it finished on time if you start later. Face facts. Procrastination is self-deception. It's denial. It's one means of lying to yourself.

But my own time management system, professionally, is still based on the crisis system. That's honesty talking. I attend to what is most pressing at the moment. Because of *experience,* I can project quite accurately how long a certain project will take.

*Dave DeBord specializes in environmental and site design. He also writes radio comedy, sitcoms, and feature films.

But I am *not* good at projecting things that go wrong or delays. So some of my crises are unexpected. And that means that the crisis system is sometimes part of my professional life.

Time management is really my only means of actually getting something done. And it requires *consistent discipline.* No time management system works without consistent discipline.

Desiree Siefkas, insurance agent who started selling insurance in 1992 and now owns her own agency:

The following are my three priority selling activities:

1. Getting potential clients to agree to receive an insurance quotation from me
2. Calling to make appointments
3. Carrying out appointments to discuss the quotations and sell insurance

I schedule time each day to ensure that I spend as much time as possible on these three activities. They are imperative for success in the insurance industry. Everything else is preparation or follow-up for these three activities.

The most important activity is number three, carrying out appointments. If I don't have an appointment, I use my time to call for appointments. If I don't have anyone to call for appointments, I use my time to line up quotations.

Afternoons and evening are for *selling activity.* No paperwork, no running errands, no taking pictures for claims, no excuses. You make money in this business by selling, not by burning gas.

Appointments to sell insurance often take place outside of traditional working hours. So I get my "business housekeeping" out of the way in the morning. I know the advice is to get the most important things done first. But this works for me. I clear the boards. My mind is clear. Then I go sell.

[*In this case, Desiree has identified her number-one priority, but she does not "get it done first." She schedules it when it can be done most effectively: when her customers are available.*]

My goal is ten quotations every day and twelve actual appointments every week. I never stop for the day until I've reached my goal. No successful agent does. But when I've reached my goal, I feel free to quit, so I'm fresh the next day.

I set those goals because of the kind of money I want to make. I want to be in six digits. These are the things I have to do to make that kind of money. In addition to the long-term goal of a six-figure income, my short-term goal is to reach a certain sales goal by May. The company whose insurance I sell provides low-interest loans to help me invest in owning my own business. If I reach certain sales goals by May of each year, I don't have to pay back the loan. Since 1992, I've never had to pay back any of the loans. This May I'll be finished with the process and will completely own my business.

My other short-term goal is to support my 15-year-old son in his basketball and other activities. I go to all the home games and games nearby. If the game is ninety minutes away, I don't go, because the drive home gets too long and too late. So some evenings I'm with my son. Other evenings I'm selling insurance.

When my batteries start running down around six at night, I go swimming at the high school. Then I have appointments in the evening or phone calls to make. It's important to me to get a lot of rest. I'm usually in bed by 10:15 p.m., watch the news, a little television, and I'm asleep.

I focus on my work. When I get off the phone with you, I'll mark everything about you as an insurance prospect. I'll fax you the quotation on your auto and homeowner's insurance tomorrow. A couple of days later, I'll call you.

[*And she did.*]

Finally, I believe in choosing which technology works for you. I got rid of call waiting because my clients didn't like being put on hold when I was asking for *their* time. Call waiting also disturbed my train of thought when I was in the middle of closing or obtaining an appointment.

I know it looks like I concentrate on money and time, but for me, it's not the money and the time—it's what you can do with them.

Robert Jordan, screenwriter and film producer:

There are at least two kinds of time management: (1) the management of what you are physically doing within any given unit of time and (2) the management of your psychological ability to focus. When I sit down to write, I know I don't have all the time in the world. But I move into another way of thinking, as if I *do* have all the time in the world. Maybe I don't have all week. Maybe I have only two days. But I write as if I have all week—as if I don't have a deadline.

I also put out of my mind every distraction, every other issue in my life. I selectively repress everything not related to the project. And then I focus. *Focused concentration is the most important time management tool available to anyone.* It achieves not only a greater quantity of work, but also a higher quality. When the focused mind and the mind at play become one and the same, the results are truly astounding. Then one draws on the total experience of a lifetime, without being thrown off by current distractions.

Recovery time is also essential. When I finish this screenplay, I will have written two movies in four months. Then I will probably take a month off. Of course, those movies were gestating for years. But the intensive writing occurred over the last four months.

When I'm writing other things that are not so intense, I also schedule recovery time. The amount of recovery time is based on what I've been doing recently. For example, if I simply go to the bank or go downtown, that's fairly mindless. I can come back and start writing. But when I work with students on Thursday nights, that's very draining. I know that all of Friday morning will be recovery time, that I'll need to just walk around the apartment listening to music or I will go out to do errands, and I will not be able to write until Friday afternoon. Helping people develop their scripts is psychologically exhausting.

When I finally sit down to write something, I finish it. Everything else gets put aside. I rarely leave a script halfway through. I will do anything to finish it. I will write fourteen, sixteen hours a day. I don't leave the apartment, I don't answer the phone, sometimes I don't shower. The only thing I'm thinking about is that screenplay.

I do not give out my private phone number. I do not give out my apartment address. I got rid of my answering machine. If I return all those phone calls, I will not write. I do not have a fax machine, and I refuse to get one. People would be faxing me scripts. And the scripts would be very hard to read. On Thursday nights, I am the servant of my students. I am all theirs. But I call them. They are not to call me. My time management includes "planned unavailability." When I need focused time, I don't take just a quiet hour. I take a quiet week. And that's what works for me.

Rosemary Kane Carlough, publisher
AMA Periodicals:

I've installed a new computerized time management system, so I didn't enter your information on my paper calendar. But I don't have my computer turned on. So I guess I'll need to go find the note I scribbled down yesterday when you called.

[*We both laughed, and, after retrieving the note, Rosemary continued to describe her time management practices.*]

I've always been very organized, even in college. After dinner, I would go to the library to study so I wouldn't be distracted. I think I might have had more fun in college if I hadn't been so organized. But now I supervise a staff of twenty-five, and I enjoy working with them.

As a supervisor, I try not to be organized to the point of compulsion. I find it extremely valuable to listen to people. It's an investment of time that can save time in the long run. I learn a lot that I would never be aware of if I merely said, "Give me the figures. Thank you. Good-bye." When the people I supervise think of me as a real human being, and we have mutual respect, (1) they come through in a pinch, (2) they work more productively every day, (3) they keep me informed, (4) they come up with great ideas, and (5) their morale is better. However, I do have ways of courteously letting them know when it's time to bring the conversation to an end.

I do not take work home—except for a couple of crunch times during the year—and I do not pull all-nighters (except on very rare occasions). Usually, I do not look at my in-box at all during the day. I take it with me to read on my fifty-minute train commute home, and I discard everything I possibly can at home, so I don't carry unnecessary paperwork back the next day and have to handle it again.

I do buy services—to buy time. I do not go to the extreme of paying someone to shop for me, but I do most of my shopping from mail order catalogues that I like. One of my husband's relatives, who lives on a farm, considers this an extravagance, given the prices in the catalog, but he does not remember the mail order heyday of Montgomery Ward on the farm. I would rather do my shopping from a catalog at 10 P.M. than give up my Saturday to spend half a day driving and the rest shopping.

I do have household help, although I've been through periods where I did it all myself. I have a person who takes care of my sons (aged 5 and 9), cleans, and cooks dinner. I value conveniences. They are worth paying for.

When I am faced with two number-one priorities, I negotiate deadlines that work for me. I would rather assert myself right up front on deadlines for a project and gain the time I need to do the work well. The other thing I do when faced with two number-one priorities is delegate. I agree with the principle that you must choose if you have two number-one priorities—and that is really what you are doing when you negotiate deadlines that work for you. You are developing a plan to accomplish one number-one priority, and then you move on to the next priority, which becomes number one.

But it's also a fact of life that you are often confronted with two priorities which both must be achieved now. This can happen with two professional priorities, but also when a number-one personal priority collides with a number-one professional priority. And whatever choices you make to deal with those situations can have very important consequences. That is why you delegate, that is why you sometimes have to negotiate deadlines, and, realistically, that is why sometimes you simply have two number-one priorities in front of you and are working on one while you take phone calls to advance progress on the other one. It's called juggling.

If you have been "downsized" and have no one to delegate to, juggling may be a necessity. Top performance provides no security in any corporate job today. The old idea that a person will have one job or career in a lifetime has given way to the certainty that everyone will be laid off at some point. It's just a question of when.

Once I grew accustomed to voice mail, I grew to love it. A lot of efficient communication can be accomplished without two people actually speaking to each other—through leaving messages on each other's machines. This actually frees up some time to allow the face-to-face encounters to be more personal.

Another thing I find very useful is having my assistant post the computer printout of my calendar on my door. It preserves communication time for important subjects rather than logistics, because my staff can check my schedule for the day without disturbing my assistant or me. Private meetings don't have to be posted. The flip side of that is that I keep another computer printout of my calendar posted on the other side of the door—in front of me—to keep me on track.

I think a very important principle is to determine what your priorities are in any situation. There are times when you decide to give extra time to a project or a client to achieve career goals or possibilities. There are other times when you decide to give extra time to an employee as an investment in that employee's skill or morale—or to achieve effective delegation. Time management is more than a cut-and-dried system. It involves thinking on your feet, as to how best to apply your principles in the given situation.

If management were as simple as it appears in business school, life would be easy. In fact, a manager is faced throughout the day with people and situations where her help is needed, and not all of these situations are predictable. Even if the help consists of helping people find the solutions themselves, it is still necessary help. The manager who only sits behind his or her door in well-organized peace is not really in tune with what is going on in the organization—and is probably not providing the most effective leadership. So an important skill is the balancing act—the ability to manage the flow and the unexpected.

Summary

As we conducted these interviews, two conclusions emerged. Each of these top time managers has applied the classic principles of time management. And each has applied them in a unique way that fits his or her own situation. The university chancellor who develops effective methods of delegating to her team, the attorney who passes on to his son a system for planning backward from the goal's deadline, the insurance salesman who lays out a time management plan with his spouse when they are in their twenties—each of these is using time management to improve their lives. But these practitioners *use* the system, rather than letting the system use them. Recognizing experience as a highly valuable tool, they view the development of their time management practices as an ongoing process and see themselves as lifelong students of the subject. The superintendent of schools, the physician at the Mayo Clinic, the pre-med student, the screenwriter, the realtor, the single parent developing a business, and the publisher have all created personal and very practical systems to make time management work for them. You can do it, too. The process can transform your life. The next step is the personal action plan.

Section B
Your Action Plan

A time log shows you the truth about what you're doing with your time. An action plan shows how you intend to make the necessary changes. Like a light bulb and a table lamp, each depends on the other for effectiveness; both are essential. In this section you can select the time concerns you want to focus your attention on; decide which of several underlying causes of each one rings especially true for you; and plot a strategy for correction, including followup.

A Systems Approach

Sometimes when people are first introduced to time management, they pounce on a specific technique or two and off they go, with little thought to overall patterns or to the ripple effect on others around them. Maybe they come across an idea in their reading or in conversation with a colleague and make a note of it. When the situation presents itself, they may or may not remember the technique; if they do, they may or may not get good results and thus may or may not try it a second time.

On their own, few people make the effort to analyze the causes of their difficulties with time management or understand the underlying principles involved. Instead, they jump to conclusions about quick and easy solutions . . . then wonder why the cure didn't "take." In a few weeks they are back to their same old ways.

People who limit their thinking to "will this help me save time," without trying to understand basic principles, will never find their way completely out of the time trap. They may save time with one technique and then *lose* it all through six other time wasters. A haphazard approach—"Gee, here's a good idea, let's try it"—will not take you far. Long-term success requires a coordinated approach, one in which overall patterns of behavior are recognized and a systematic plan for improvement is sketched out and methodically implemented.

Do not, that is to say, limit yourself to a few "whats"; go for understanding the "whys." *Then* select the "whats" that match the "whys." This way lies success.

Setting the Stage for Strategic Action

Your first step is to decide which time concerns to work on, based on what you learned about yourself in your time log (see Chapter Four) and the twenty self-audits in Part Two. Step one: Develop your own personal target list of ten problem areas.

The self-audits, you may remember, are structured in a positive scoring mode. That is, the higher your score on an audit, the better your time practices in that particular area. So go back through Part Two and list the ten audits you scored *lowest* on. Rank them in sequence, starting with the lowest score first; those are your ten biggest time concerns.

Now review your time log side by side with your "top ten" list. Take what you learned about your behavior patterns from the time log, and express that self-knowledge in terms of the twenty time concerns. You may have some questions about which time waster a particular action on the time log should be attributed to. Suppose you realize that you lost time on a certain day because you were working on a project you should not have been doing in the first place. Is that poor delegation, inability to say no to interruptions, or perhaps lack of priorities? Don't agonize over it; remember that there is a considerable amount of interconnection, and even some overlap, between time wasters. There should be a reasonably close correlation between the audit-derived list and the revelations of the time log, but it's not essential that the two match exactly.

Organize Your Approach

The next step is to rank your top ten in a sequence of attack. Which time concern should you solve first? Some people prefer to start with their number-one problem, on the theory that that will provide the greatest gain. Others, sensing the danger of defeat, elect to start with the area they believe will be the easiest to solve, thus ensuring a success right off the bat. It is really a matter of individual choice, based on your own psychology and personal work style.

Then decide on a structure for your plan. These two seem to work best for most people:

1. The One-a-Week Plan, in which you concentrate solely on one time waster a week; this is a ten-week program.
2. The Three-Month Plan, in which you work each month on a group of three or four problems: three in months one and two, four in month three.

In the first case, you put all your attention on one time concern for a full week, and make a concerted effort to change your habits in that one area. Then move on to the next one. In the second case, you will focus on three at the same time, and then next month move on to three (or four) others. People who like the immediate success factor of short-range objectives usually prefer the first; the second method works well for those who can find connecting links to their time problems and so can easily work on several at one time.

Whichever way you choose, start by recording your list of ten on an Action Plan Worksheet like the one shown in Figure 14. Let's suppose your first three items are ineffective delegation, drop-in visitors, and meetings.

Getting to the Bottom of Things

Now begin integrating the information in Part Two. Review the descriptions for your top time wasters. Do you see yourself in any of the situations described there? Can you relate to the discussion of basic causes? Isolating the real causes of your biggest time concerns is the next important step.

The self-audits for each time waster can help you narrow things down. Look again at the individual questions, and put a big red star by the ones you scored lowest on. This is where you need to put your attention.

Figure 14. Action Plan Worksheet, Part 1.

Time Barrier	Cause	Solution
1. delegation	I think I can do it better myself.	Get off ego trip! Realize value of training others.
2. drop-in visitors	open-door policy	Redefine meaning of "open". Establish quiet times.
3. meetings	I attend meetings I shouldn't.	Ask WT to excuse me from meetings not relevant to my job.

Making the Change

Now you have the exciting challenge of coming up with solutions. Well, you're in for a welcome surprise: Nearly every cause suggests its own solution. For example, lack of planning is one of the most common causes of time problems. Its solution—no surprise here—is planning. Of course, some additional detail is needed to make this solution meaningful to your particular situation.

Keep these basic, simple solutions in mind as you look to the help provided by the many ideas presented throughout Part Two and in Appendix A. Write down the solution, or solutions, for your main causes. In many cases, the solutions suggested are general. It's up to you to turn them into specific action points in your own life. Have some fun with this; dream a bit. If you could design the perfect work setting, one where time wasters wither and die from lack of nutrients, what would you do? Even goofy ideas have value if they trigger other creative solutions. One word of caution, though: Make sure you are thinking of things *you* can do; don't merely dump your problems on someone else.

Here's a review of the sequence so far, with one example:

1. Choose a time waster to work on: drop-in visitors.
2. Find a relative cause: open-door policy.
3. What solution goes with that cause: redefine open door.
4. Brainstorm possible action steps, even silly ones:

   —Talk to RER; can we rephrase the official statement of policy?
   —Paint the door red so everyone can see when it's closed.
   —Charge $1 toll for anyone who comes in when it's closed.
   —Move Claire's desk so they have to climb over it.
   —Move my desk to face the window, not the doorway.
   —Start quiet hour in the whole department.

Then, from all your ideas, select the most workable and write them down on Part 2 of your Action Plan Worksheet as action steps (see Figure 15). Then designate a start date, the specific day on which you will institute each change. Then do it.

Learning New Habits

Planning some new ways of doing things is relatively easy; sticking with them is something else again. You may remember that in Chapter One we talked about the remarkable force called habit. As you begin to manage yourself and your time differently, you will no doubt find yourself bumping up against some old habits. Yes, habits are very strong, and very tough. But so are you.

To reinforce your new behavior, use these ideas, first suggested by the nineteenth-century American psychologist, William James.

1. *Think big.* Give your new habits every chance for success by launching them strongly. Set up a new routine that contrasts with the old one. Create whatever reminders and visual prompts you wish. Announce your new plans to as many people as you appropriately can; this public declaration will motivate you to stay on track. Work out a "buddy" arrangement with a colleague; you agree to meet regularly and check each other's progress. In short, surround your resolution with every aid you know. This gives you momentum against the temptation to backslide.

2. *Practice the new habit often.* Seize the first possible chance to act out your new methods. Resolutions communicate a new "set" to the brain—not when they are formed but when they produce motor effects. Repetition will ingrain the new behavior; merely thinking about it will not.

3. *Don't make exceptions.* A lapse is like a skid in a car. It takes much more effort to recover control than to maintain it from the outset. A slip can diminish the energy of all future attempts. Whenever you say, "I'll make an exception just this once," your carefully crafted plan will begin to crumble.

When Others Are Involved

If you want to reclaim some of the time you now waste by procrastinating, you can make significant progress by setting firm

Figure 15. Action Plan Worksheet, Part 2.

Solution	Action Steps	Start Date
Realize value in training others.	① Teach Claire to answer all routine price inquiries — never do it again!	10-1
	② Turn sales summary responsibility over to Michael; review monthly.	10-3
	③ Put Elise in charge of leotard line; take her to studio.	10-3
Redefine "open door" to mean "accessible"	① Set up quiet hour 9-10; explain to Claire and rest of department	10-12
	② Talk to RER about restating policy companywide	10-8
	③ Move desk to face away from doorway	10-3
Skip meetings not related to my job	① Practice asking MEK about sales force meeting	10-1
	② Always ask for agenda if not provided; see where I fit	10-1
	③ Ask if I can send written ideas instead	10-4

deadlines on yourself. Success or failure with this particular solution is totally in your hands. But if you plan to shift the weekly
sales report to Thursday afternoon so you can do higher-priority
projects earlier in the week, you had better be sure to inform all
those who are accustomed to receiving it on Tuesday.

You are in charge of your time, but your actions and decisions can affect others. One woman who took a time management seminar and learned about the quiet hour put this idea
into practice the very next day—without explaining to anyone
why she was making herself unavailable for an hour each morning. Her boss was upset and her assistant was confused and frustrated as were others accustomed to walking through the open
door. The lesson here is simple: If you make a change that affects
other people, warn them.

The question is much more complex when the problem de-
rives from other people's actions. As part of your action plan,
determine when your particular time wasters are caused by you
alone—and therefore can be solved with individual effort. If others are involved, you will need a team approach.

Time and Teams

No resource is as team-oriented as time. A meeting that never
should have been called wastes the time of all who get stuck in
it. A disorganized person who fails to produce requested information on time directly affects the persons who need the
information—to say nothing of those further along the communication chain. Supervisors who do not delegate effectively
lower everyone's productivity—and morale. A "team" approach
to time is necessary in situations like this. The root of the difficulty involves others in the organization, and changing only
your own behavior won't fully solve the problem.

Managers and supervisors must be keenly alert here. When
ineffective use of time affects only your work, that's one thing
(although it is bad enough). But when it interferes with the work
that others must do, the loss to the organization is much greater.
A newly promoted division manager in a major communications company called frequent meetings of his top team because

he felt insecure in the new assignment. Meeting after meeting he would pump the entire team, sometimes for as long as four hours, for information that would help him perform his job. One person was destroying the effectiveness of an entire group.

What is needed here is a coordinated effort. If everyone can obtain training in time management as a group, this is ideal. When all members of the team are exposed to the same concepts and techniques, they reinforce each other in a way that significantly enhances the end results. Experienced trainers have estimated the improved results at ten times the original.

If outside training is not possible, a strong person in the team must take charge. Try to assemble the group for a brainstorming session on the particular problem. As a group, pinpoint specific behaviors, identify the underlying causes of those behaviors, and devise strategies for correction, along with start dates.

If, as is likely, there are multiple problems, this same person can lead the group toward team-oriented time management solutions. Get the team together, have everyone list and rank main individual time wasters; then assign a weight to each, and consolidate the lists to reveal a team profile. (Figure 16 illustrates the process.) Then, using the same steps described earlier for individuals—but working as a team—define basic solutions and then create specific action steps with time lines.

Making It Work

We all recognize the early enthusiasm that accompanies new ideas, and the frustration and disappointment we feel as determination dribbles away. To keep your plan on track, and your good intentions intact, review these three essentials:

1. *Commitment to definite actions.* Unless your plans are specific and concrete, it will be difficult to translate them into actual practice. General notions tend to stay general. Also, unless you are committed to putting your plans into effect, nothing will happen. As with all habits, the first step is to take clear, definite actions to establish them.

Figure 16. Team profile of time concerns.

Instructions:

1. Select your top ten time wasters by assigning weights in descending order of importance. Give your top time waster a weight of 10, your next most important 9, etc.:

Your Rank		Weight		Your Rank		Weight
1	=	10		6	=	5
2	=	9		7	=	4
3	=	8		8	=	3
4	=	7		9	=	2
5	=	6		10	=	1

Record weights in column A.

2. Record *weights* for the time wasters for each team member in columns B through D.

3. Total the weights for each time waster in column W.

4. Establish a *ranking* by weights in column R to obtain your team profile. The largest weight ranks no. 1, etc.

Rank of My Time Wasters

Rank		Time Waster	A	B	C	D	W	R
2	1.	Management by crisis	9	8	4		21	2
6	2.	Telephone interruptions	5	10	9		24	1
	3.	Inadequate planning						
1	4.	Attempting too much	10		3		13	6
	5.	Drop-in visitors		5	10		15	4
5	6.	Ineffective delegation	6	7	5		18	3
3	7.	Personal disorganization	8	6			14	5
	8.	Lack of self-discipline		2	7		9	10
	9.	Inability to say no		3	2		5	12
	10.	Procrastination		4	6		10	9
7	11.	Meetings	4		8		12	7
10	12.	Paper work	1	9	1		11	8
	13.	Leaving tasks unfinished						
4	14.	Inadequate staff	7				7	11
	15.	Socializing		1			1	15
	16.	Confused responsibility						
9	17.	Poor communication	2				2	14
	18.	Inadequate controls						
8	19.	Incomplete information	3				3	13
	20.	Travel						

© 1987 Alec Mackenzie

2. *Continued, consistent effort.* A new habit needs practice and a firm stand against exceptions. You must return periodically to evaluate your progress, take note of lapses, and initiate corrective action. A minimum period of three months is needed for a good evaluation; one year is better.

3. *Group action.* Many of your failures are the result of pressure from others (clients, colleagues, and so on) who expect you to continue your former way of responding. The best step toward breaking this expectation is to get a commitment from the group on major actions. Always communicate your plans to those who will be affected by them and try to get their consent to respect these changes.

Followup and Reinforcement

• *After one month.* Review the progress you have made in the first month. Where did you succeed? Where did you slip? Analyze what went wrong. Go back and review the three steps for breaking old habits. Decide where additional reinforcement is needed. List the steps you will take. Then go on to your next group of time wasters.

• *After three months.* Whether you are doing one time waster a week, or three per month, at the end of three months you should have completed your action plan for your top ten problem areas. How did you do? Keep a time log again for three days. Measure the time saved, and your improved results.

• *Long-range followup.* To avoid the danger of regression, I recommend you take a time log once a quarter (to check on how you're doing). Some people do it continually, to take advantage of its self-correcting properties.

If at any of these followup points you discover that a certain time waster is proving particularly stubborn, and you just can't seem to get it under control, you may need a concentrated effort on that one item. Start by keeping a targeted time log for a few days. Keep track of all instances of the specific problem, and then analyze what is happening and how you might correct it.

Figure 17 is Chris's targeted time log for drop-in visitors;

Figure 17. Chris's targeted time log.

Time Waster Target: _drop-in visitors_

Goal: _to reduce interruptions from items that have lower priority than task at hand_

Priority: 1—Most Important; 2—Less Important; 3—Routine, Detail; 4—Trivia

Analysis: Be sure to note.time lost in recovering concentration after an interruption occurs.

Date: __12/20__

Time	Call In/Out	Who, What	Time Used	Priority	Activity Interrupted	Priority	Analysis
10:37		Boss, hol. Sched.	15	4	sales rept.	1	find way to cut short
11:15		Boss, sales rept.	15	1	paperwork	3	boss found mistake
11:45		Secty — Red Cross	1	4	collecting data for launch mtg.	2	secty could consult list
2:30		George — discuss ball games	2	4	prep for plng mtg.	1	suggested coffee, accepted
3:45		Mgr. on plant safety	45	4	new product launch prep	2	should have begged off—not my area

244

the form will work for any sort of interruption—crises, visitors, phone calls, paperwork, unexpected meetings—the problems that are usually the peskiest.

Making Time Work for You
and Your Organization

Breaking out of the time trap is a challenging, invigorating experience. As you begin to make progress in cutting away some of the barriers, you will see real changes in your overall well-being. Some may be dramatic, others less obvious. But one day you recognize that you're no longer drowning in chaos by 11:00 every morning, and that you're not totally exhausted by 5:00 in the afternoon. Before long you're going home on time, leaving with a sense of having accomplished real work instead of spinning your wheels, and you are *not* taking your briefcase with you.

Having learned to better manage your use of time, you have:

- Reduced your stress level
- Improved your productivity level
- Made progress toward your goals
- Achieved a healthy balance between your personal and professional worlds

And lest anyone doubt it, skillful time management also has tremendous bottom-line significance to your organization. In their very first month of new time practices, one group of 124 managers in one of the world's largest chemical companies actually saved the annual equivalent of more than $1 million in time. (In fact, the true total was even higher, for some who had taken the training did not return their data to be included in the tally.) Here's how the numbers look.

Through time management training, these managers saved, on average, one and a quarter hours a day. With an annual average salary of $50,000 (plus benefits), that translates to $1,259,375 savings for the company.

Hours per day per person	1.25
Work days per year	× 250
Hours per person per year	312.5
Average compensation per hour	× $32.50
Annual value of time saved per person	
	$10,156.25
People	× 124
Annual value of total time saved	$1,259,375.00

My studies over many years consistently indicate that, on average, people can save *two hours* a day with better time habits. That's ten hours a week, five hundred hours a year. Just imagine if each person in your organization was magically given five hundred extra hours each year; how much more successful could the company be?

As you're heading home—at a reasonable hour, for a change—think about this. Think, too, of how much you are looking forward to being home, with all the warmth and sustenance it provides you, now that you are not as stressed as you used to be. Success in your personal life, success in your business life— you now have time for both.

Appendix A

Escaping the Time Trap: Summary of the Twenty Biggest Time Wasters and Their Causes and Solutions

Attempting Too Much

Causes	Solutions
1. Unaware of importance	Take three-day time log. Analyze tendency to take on things your team and others could be doing. Delegate more and say no when appropriate.
2. Lack of priorities and planning	Set objectives, priorities, deadlines in four critical time frames (daily, weekly, monthly, and yearly). Focus on top priorities and ignore the bulk of activities that contribute nothing to your objectives.
3. Unrealistic time estimates	Recognize that everything takes longer than you think (Murphy's Second Law). Analyze characteristic underestimates, then add appropriate cushion to all critical estimates (20 to 50 percent). Develop the habit of asking yourself, "What was the result of the activity I just completed?"
4. Responding to the urgent	Distinguish the urgent from the truly important. Balance short-term objectives. Ask "What's the worst that can happen?" before responding.

Causes	*Solutions*
5. Overresponse	Limit your response to the real demands of the situation. Stay uninvolved if others can handle it. Delegate if subordinates can handle situation.
6. Overambition and inordinate need to achieve	Control your ambition to fit your abilities and situation. Ask yourself what you are trying to prove. Be realistic; keep perspective. Stop killing yourself. Recognize that if you unrealistically attempt too much, you may not achieve anything. Determine what you really want to achieve, focus on that, and learn to live with the fact that you will have regrets no matter what.
7. Desire to impress boss	Discuss what boss really wants. Recognize that long-term success is more important to bosses than short-term impressions.
8. Overdesire to appear cooperative	Stop saying yes just because you want to be appreciated. Recognize difference between being cooperative and doing others' work. Learn to say no without offending. Use your own priorities as reasons and offer alternatives when appropriate.
9. Understaffed	Expose staff to time management and target saving two hours a day for each person. Do feasibility study with time log to demonstrate that actual additional help would be cost-effective.
10. Perfectionism	Lower standards to what is reasonable. Allocate time frames more closely.

Communication, Poor

Causes	*Solutions*
1. Unaware of importance	Recognize. Read relevant sections of this book and take audits.
2. Lack of time	Take the time. Priority warrants.
3. Not listening/inattentive	Develop and practice listening skills.

Causes	Solutions
4. Purpose not clear	Clarify. Assess before the communication what you want to accomplish. Jot down notes on paper or in your computer.
5. Use of wrong channel	Select appropriate channel (phone, letter, memo, conference).
6. Poor timing	Select appropriate time.
7. Insufficient communication	Assess legitimate needs for information. Provide through staff meetings, organization publications, memoranda.
8. Lack of receptivity	Test receptivity: "Would you like to talk about. . . . ?"
9. Differing value systems	Recognize that experience, training, and environment create different backgrounds for interpreting communication.
10. Lack of feedback	Get feedback to ensure understanding. Take corrective action.

Confused Responsibility or Authority

Causes	Solutions
1. Failure to clarify precise responsibility with manager or partner	Prepare list of responsibilities for manager's or partner's approval.
2. Lack of position/job description	Write one. Discuss with boss. Get approved. Include both responsibilities and authority.
3. Job description overlaps others	Identify areas of duplication. Eliminate.
4. Usurping of authority by others	Identify. Discuss with boss. Clarify. Insist that if authority in doubt, then responsibility must be limited to match.
5. Responsibility without authority	Insist on commensurate authority (equal to responsibility). It is mandatory to have the power (authority) to carry out one's duty (responsibility).
6. Nondescriptive titles	Titles convey apparent authority to the world in which we work. They must be descriptive of real authority to avoid confusion.
7. Confused or no	Organization charts provide the skeleton for

Causes	*Solutions*
organization chart	authority relationships and are essential to clarify lines of responsibility and authority within the organization.
8. Generic job descriptions	Develop specific job description, detailed, to cover individual responsibilities.
9. Lack of emphasis on assumption of responsibility and exercise of initiative	Emphasize through accountability for result, recognition and reward for hard work, citation, consideration in performance and salary review, promotion, etc.
10. Employees unwilling to accept responsibility	Management should select people with care. Train. Reward.

Delegation, Ineffective

Causes	*Solutions*
1. Insecurity/fear of failure	Recognize. Accept risk as inherent. Accept mistakes; learn from them.
2. Lack confidence in staff	Train, develop, trust. Use progress reports for control.
3. Giving unclear, incomplete, or confused instructions	Ensure clear, complete, unambiguous instructions. Ask subordinate to repeat, ensuring understanding.
4. Can do the job better and faster yourself	Lower standards to what is acceptable, not your own level of performance. Avoid perfectionism.
5. More comfortable "doing" than "managing"	Recognize that practice leads to success, which leads to comfort. Remember the job of the manager is managing, not doing.
6. Expect everyone to know all the details	Recognize that this should not be expected of someone who has delegated responsibility for handling.
7. Failure to establish appropriate controls	Establish plans, schedules with details, progress reports, monitoring of deadlines.
8. Overcontrol	Relax. Emphasize goal-accomplishment, not methods and procedures. Measure results, not activity.

Causes	Solutions
9. Failure to fol-lowup	Always check progress in time to take correc-tive action.
10. Understaffed/overworked sub-ordinates	Limit expectations and reduce accepted re-sponsibilities.
11. No one to dele-gate to	Establish trade-offs with co-workers. If you are self-employed, form temporary partner-ships, trade services, and assess whether you need to put the arrangement in writing.

Drop-In Visitors

Causes	Solutions
1. No plan for han-dling	Develop plan to screen. Arrange appoint-ments.
2. Ego, feeling of importance	Recognize. Don't overestimate importance to others of your availability. Plan social visits at coffee or lunch.
3. Desire to be avail-able	Distinguish between being available for busi-ness and for socializing.
4. No plans for un-availability	Modified open door; quiet hour; screening; hideaway.
5. Fear of offending	Don't be oversensitive.
6. Open-door policy	Recognize "open door" does not mean physi-cally open, but open to those who need as-sistance. Modify your open door by closing it regularly for periods of concentration. Re-define "open" to mean "accessible." Quiet hour is best.
7. Requiring or ex-pecting subordi-nates to check with you exces-sively	Manage by exception. Expect information concerning only deviations from plan. Schedule regular meetings daily or weekly to handle multiple items arising between meetings.
8. Inability to termi-nate visits	Go to the office of others. Meet them outside your office. Stand up upon entry and keep standing. Preset time limit on visit. Fore-shadow end ("Is there anything else before I leave?"). Assistant interrupts to remind

Causes	*Solutions*
	you of an urgent matter. Be candid ("I'm sorry, I must get back to other matters now"). Stand up and walk to door.
9. Boss, persistent friends	Develop subtle techniques. Remind boss of something you have to do for him or her. Appear busy. Be candid.
10. Poor physical location, heavy traffic pattern; exposed, without door or personal office	Change if possible. If not, concentrate; avoid eye contact. Take log to show management what interruptions are costing. Find hideaway to take quiet hour.
11. Client's desire to be helpful	Explain that you will both have more time to devote to the project if the client "drops off" material in a predetermined physical location such as a slot or a box to receive documents.

Inability to Say No

Causes	*Solutions*
1. Desire to win approval, acceptance	Recognize possible trap. If desired results are not achieved, you may lose instead of gain respect and feel resentful.
2. Fear of offending	True friends are not offended by honest explanations. Develop techniques of saying no without offending. Examples: "Thanks for the compliment, but I'll have to decline." "Sorry I can't, but let me offer a suggestion. . . ."
3. Possess capabilities in demand	Recognize this asset makes ability to say no even more imperative. Refuse to spread yourself too thin. Concentrate your efforts.
4. False sense of obligation	Recognize prevalence of this cause. Examine reasons for this feeling. Discuss with family, friends, associates. Control.
5. Not knowing how to refuse	*Listen* to the request. Say *no* at once if appropriate to do so. Give *reasons*. Suggest *alternatives*.

Causes	*Solutions*
6. Lack excuses	Don't be too sensitive. Sometimes no excuse is better than a poor one. Think of acceptable excuses ahead of time. Best excuse is your own priorities. Keep them visible on your daily plan.
7. No time to think of answer or excuse	Count to ten before saying yes. Give yourself time. Delay response.
8. Lack objectives and priorities	Others will determine priorities for you if you don't have your own. Then, whatever you achieve will be determined by your environment, not by you.
9. Thoughtless assumption by others that you will say yes	Recognize that you have likely encouraged this assumption by never saying no. Learn to say no, especially to inappropriate or thoughtless requests or those that will make you feel bad if you assent.
10. Can't say no to boss	Say no by showing list of agreed-upon priorities. If boss insists, acquiesce, but advise what you fear will not get done.

Information, Incomplete

Causes	*Solutions*
1. Unaware of importance	Recognize and assign priority.
2. Lack system	Determine what information is needed for planning, decisions, and feedback on results. Then ensure its availability, reliability, and timeliness. Also determine which information is *not* needed. Information overload will bog you down. Develop the habit of making this assessment at the beginning of every task and of reassessing your information requirements as you progress through the task.
3. Difficult to know what information is needed	Discuss and decide.

Causes	*Solutions*
4. Failure to test its reliability	Make no assumptions. Too critical. Test periodically.
5. Providing information not needed or requested	Avoid unnecessary communication. Stick to essentials. Avoid overkill.
6. Failure to assess priority or urgency of requested information	Make assessment and allocate time accordingly. Standardize priority of information classifications.
7. Failure to anticipate probable delays in obtaining information	Expect delays. Plan accordingly. Build in a cushion of time to compensate. Identify alternate sources if possible.
8. Lack of authority to require information needed	Clarify authority. Use response deadlines. Take problem to boss if unsuccessful.
9. Indecision or delay by others in providing needed information	"Unless I hear" memo. Meet to explain importance of information.
10. Support staff uninformed	Schedule regular meetings with managers. Ask to be included in informational staff meetings.

Leaving Tasks Unfinished

Causes	*Solutions*
1. Unaware of the problem	Take time log. Assess impact of leaving tasks unfinished (number, length of interruption, importance of tasks left unfinished).
2. Lack objectives, priorities, and deadlines	Set objectives and arrange in order of importance to clarify those things that ought to be finished first. Set deadlines on all important tasks to provide incentive to complete them.
3. Failure to reward self	Reward yourself with a list of items to be crossed off, by deferring pleasant diversions

Causes	Solutions
	until certain tasks are completed, etc.
4. Responding to the urgent	Recognize that urgent matters rarely are as important as they seem. Resist tendency to overreact, thus interrupting other tasks. Keep priorities visible for ready excuse to say no to interruptions.
5. Cluttered desk/ personal disorganization	Get organized to permit effective control of tasks. Be systematic in handling information. Recognize that sound organization saves time in retrieving information, processing decisions, and completing tasks.
6. Lack determination to complete tasks (lack self-discipline, lazy)	Impose deadlines on yourself and announce them to others (go public). Employ assistance (e.g., have assistant remind you to ensure task's accomplishment). Monitor progress.
7. Inability to delegate	Delegate task completion to somebody else.
8. Accepting interruptions	Have interruptions screened. Establish quiet hour for completing tasks. *Always* note the amount of time it takes you *after* the interruption to refocus on the original task. This becomes a self-training mechanism that prevents you from accepting interruptions in the future.
9. Shifting priorities	Keep priorities current (reprioritize). Measure relative importance of new demands against current priorities. Resist unnecessary changes and resulting loss of time in leaving and later resuming tasks.
10. Incomplete or unreliable information blocks task completion	Recognize need for adequate information and ensure its availability before starting tasks.

Management by Crisis

Causes	Solutions
1. Unaware of importance	Take time log of crises. Analyze source, causes, seriousness, controllable factors.

Causes	*Solutions*
2. Failure to antici-pate problems and to develop contingency plans	Expect the unexpected. Ask what can go wrong. (Murphy's Third Law: If anything can go wrong, it will.) List potential problems. Categorize by seriousness and probability, then develop steps to prevent if possible, or to limit consequences if not.
3. Overreaction (treating problems as crises)	Limit your response by (a) ignoring problems which can be ignored; (b) delegating all those which others can handle; (c) handling only those which you alone can take care of.
4. Fire fighting	Recognize that it is more important to prevent new fires from developing than to spend all your time putting out old ones. Preventive action is preferable to remedial.
5. Procrastination	Recognize danger inherent in putting off key actions: leads to deadline pressures and often to impaired judgment under stress.
6. Unrealistic time estimates	Recognize that everything takes longer than you think it will (Murphy's Second Law). Analyze characteristic underestimates, then add appropriate cushion to all critical estimates, at least 20 percent.
7. Mechanical breakdown/ human error	Anticipate. Organize resources (human and otherwise) for rapid adjustments to compensate most effectively. Back up your computer files and your databases. Install a utilities program to detect and repair computer errors *before* they cause crises.
8. Reluctance of staff to break bad news	Develop philosophy of mistakes (learning process). Discuss; emphasize that fast reporting of bad news will help prevent crises.
9. Overreaction engendered by VIP request	Find out *what* really is wanted, by *whom, when* it really is needed, and *how* it will be used. Are there any alternatives?
10. Failure to establish controls	Timeline all major projects. Establish checkpoints at intervals to confirm targets are being met.

Meetings

Causes	Solutions
1. Lack of purpose	No meeting without a purpose; in writing if possible.
2. Lack of agenda	No meeting without an agenda. Written agenda for scheduled meeting; verbal agenda if unscheduled to ensure that people come prepared.
3. Wrong people/ too many/to few	Only those needed should attend.
4. No planning	Allow for and schedule appropriate planning for most effective meeting.
5. Too many/too few meetings	Test need for regular meetings. Occasionally don't hold one; see what happens. Or cut time allowed in half for those tending to last a long time. Assess need for participation, information, and coordination. Schedule accordingly. Hold the meeting by computer, with a chairperson conducting the meeting. Hold the meeting by using three-way calling, teleconferencing, video conferencing, or fiber optics. Or skip the meeting entirely and use e-mail.
6. Not starting/ ending on time	Start and end on time. By delaying for late arrivals, the leader penalizes those who arrive on time and rewards those who come late! By ending late, the leader prevents attendees from making other plans—or loses attendees who walk out.
7. Allowing interruptions	Set policy and let everyone know. Whenever possible, allow no interruptions except for real emergency. Hold messages until breaks of long meetings and after short meetings.
8. Wandering from agenda	Expect and demand adherence to agenda. Resist "hidden agenda" ploys.
9. Failure to summarize conclusions	Summarize conclusions to ensure agreement and remind participants of assignments.
10. Failure to followup	Ensure effective followup on all decisions in meeting minutes. List uncompleted items under "Unfinished Business" at beginning

Causes	*Solutions*
	of next agenda. Request status reports until completed.

Paperwork

Causes	*Solutions*
1. Indecision	Read it once, and handle it.
2. Procrastination	Do it now. Eighty percent of daily intake can be disposed of on first handling. The average manager disposes of only 20 percent.
3. Not delegating	Do nothing you can delegate. Divorce yourself from detail and routine. Remember paper follows responsibility that has been delegated.
4. Perfectionism	"Is it adequate?" (not perfect) should be your standard.
5. Hoarding	Get rid of it; keep it moving.
6. Overfiling	Code dictation to indicate filing life: P = Permanent M = Medium T = Temporary. Answer on original when copy not essential. If filing is necessary, use back of original for copy of your response.
7. Leaving tasks unfinished	Complete tasks before putting them down.
8. Attempting too much at once	Be realistic.
9. Lack system	Develop system for simplifying paperwork: reduce copies; standardize forms; use computer templates and macros; reduce report length and number where possible; screen selectively; delegate; file selectively, alphabetically, and with cross references; control record retention; include name of paper file with electronic file.
10. Slow reader	Screen and select with discrimination. Scan for essentials. Take a speed-reading course. Have assistant summarize content.

Personal Disorganization

Causes	Solutions
1. Unaware of importance	Recognize stacked desk as major interrupter and cause of lost documents (retrieval time). Take time log to assess retrieval time.
2. Lack of system	Use organizer system to record things you wish to remember so documents may be filed away.
3. Ego (viewed by some as a symbol of busyness, importance, indispensability)	Recognize excessive paper may also symbolize personal disorganization, indecision, procrastination, insecurity, confusion of priorities. Find better method of control than keeping all files on desk.
4. Fear loss of control	Use project plan sheets to provide better control than keeping all files on a cluttered desk.
5. Fear of forgetting	Proper calendaring and use of contact logs will be excellent memory substitute. No need to remember what can be retrieved.
6. Allowing interruptions	Screen; set aside "time banks" for planned unavailability to complete your work. Try to delay even important interruptions long enough to complete task you are on.
7. Procrastination/ indecision	Tackle toughest, highest-priority tasks first. Self impose deadlines and reward yourself. Eighty percent of tasks coming to your desk can be handled at once. Do it now. Keep the paper moving.
8. Lack objectives, priorities, and daily plan	Recognize that poor planning causes indecision, switching priorities, and leaving tasks unfinished. Plan your work. Work your plan.
9. Failure to delegate	Do nothing you can delegate. You not only overload yourself with others' work but deny them experience.
10. Failure to screen	Staff screens out junk mail, refers requests others can handle, prepares responses for own or your signature.
11. Failure to use available tools	Research paper and electronic contact management systems, including personal digital assistants, and determine if one can meet your needs. Then *learn* to use its features.

Planning, Inadequate

Causes	Solutions
1. Unaware of importance	Recognize that every hour in effective planning saves three to four in execution and gets better results.
2. Lack system	Develop; include plan sheet, daily objectives, priorities, and deadlines. Use an integrated system, by hand or by computer.
3. Lack time to plan	Take it. Assign it the priority it deserves. Recognize that planning takes time initially, but pays off with better results in less time.
4. Crisis-oriented (assumes crises are unavoidable)	Recognize fallacy. Except for acts of God, most crises are relatively predictable. Allow more time. Plan ahead for contingencies.
5. Lack self-discipline	Impose deadlines on yourself. Try objectives, priorities, and daily plan for one month. Enlist aid of associates. Monitor progress. Evaluate results.
6. Fear of commitment	Recognize that while objectives mean commitment, they also mean knowing when you have succeeded.
7. Lack of job description	Recognize objectives are easier to develop when key result areas are clearly identified.
8. Difficulty of assigning priorities to tasks	Not easy, but one of the most productive of all managerial pursuits. Determines where efforts should be concentrated. Identify three criteria for priorities (long-range importance, short-range urgency, growth trend). List your objectives and rank them according to those criteria.
9. Assumption that since few days are "typical," it is futile to plan, or that emergencies will spoil plans anyway	Recognize that most managers tend to waste time in the same or similar ways every day. And while emergencies may disrupt a day, the damage can be minimized more easily if the day was planned and the most vital tasks completed before or returned to after the emergency.
10. Have plan in mind but believe it is not important enough to write it down	Recognize that no memory is infallible, and that no to-do list is complete until priorities and deadlines are set.

Procrastination

Causes	Solutions
1. Inability to identify	Procrastination means putting off or delaying without justification. Ask others to help you identify instances.
2. Ego trip (crisis creating)	Recognize tendency to allow a crisis to develop so you can assume the role of "hero" in solving it. Anticipate cost of pressure/crisis syndrome.
3. Thinking I "work best under pressure"	Recognize this assumption is pure rationalization. Get number one done first!
4. Habit of doing the easy or trivial first, postponing the difficult	Recognize great danger here—that what we may not get done is the most vital. Pressure and crises usually result. Get number one done first!
5. Unrealistic time estimates	Recognize everything takes longer than you think (Murphy's Second Law). Build in 20 to 50 percent cushion on all major tasks. Leave 20 percent of your day unplanned (unscheduled) to compensate for underestimates.
6. Attempting too much	This ensures some things won't get done. Prioritize your goals to get the most important things done.
7. Lack regular monitoring of progress	This encourages leaving whole jobs until the last minute, practically guaranteeing a crisis. Fast feedback on progress provides motivation to improve and alerts you if you are falling behind schedule. Have an assistant check your progress against deadlines at regular intervals.
8. Lack of self-discipline	Use all available techniques: setting deadlines on all objectives and priorities; going public; asking help in monitoring progress; submitting regular progress reports (even if not requested); establishing reminders (list, egg timer, wrist alarm); rewarding yourself.
9. Leaving tasks unfinished	Usually takes much less time and effort to complete a task than to have to come back and attempt to finish it when the details have become blurred. Finish it the first time

Causes	Solutions
	to prevent procrastination becoming an issue!
10. Lack of deadlines	Recognize deadlines are one of your most valuable tools. They provide a sense of urgency as well as a means for measuring progress. Deadline every major task.
11. Fear that the task will be too difficult	Divide the task into very small steps and complete the first step. Note your success and then complete the second very small step.
12. Fear of boredom	Identify the value the completed task will have for you personally.

Progress Reports, Inadequate Controls and

Causes	Solutions
1. Unaware of importance	Recognize that controls, like thermostats, monitor progress and correct variance, thus guaranteeing satisfactory performance.
2. Lack of familiarity with tools	Review timeline and Project Plan Sheet.
3. Belief that sound plans somehow achieve themselves	Recognize that "best-laid plans" are nothing more than that: plans.
4. Lack enforcement of controls and progress reports now in place	Recognize this means you might as well not have them.

Self-Discipline, Lack of

Causes	Solutions
1. Lack objectives or standards	Set objectives in key result areas, both personal and organizational. Develop standards (conditions that will exist when the job is done well) for routine tasks.

Causes	*Solutions*
2. Lack of planning and priorities	Set priorities to focus effort on most productive areas. This ensures that what gets done will be most important . . . and what doesn't get done is least important. Develop plans to achieve your priorities.
3. Not setting deadlines	Impose realistic but firm deadlines on all major tasks. Expect them of others.
4. Not following up	Recognize that people do what you inspect, not what you expect—and the same goes for you. So check your results against your plan. Are you progressing according to schedule? Have an assistant or associate monitor your progress.
5. Not using available tools and techniques	Evaluate and use such aids as daily written plan, deadlines, PERT charts, progress reports, project control charts, and weekly plan sheets.
6. Lack of interest	Reexamine attitude toward job. Recognize that indifference makes self-discipline more difficult. Set demanding goals to generate interest and motivation. Answer the questions "What do I want professionally and personally? What steps do I need to take to get from where I am to where I want to be?" Without creating this real motivation for yourself, discipline will always be an uphill battle.
7. Leaving tasks unfinished	Recognize wasted effort in stopping and restarting tasks. Economy of effort dictates completing tasks before putting them down. Handle it once. Get it done the first time.
8. Daydreaming	Learn the art of concentration and practice it. Avoid distractions and self-interruptions.
9. Procrastination	Identify tasks and decisions subject to procrastination. Set realistic deadlines. Go public by announcing them. Use assistant to help you monitor results. Reward yourself when successful. *Identify* your fear that the task may be difficult. Divide the task into very small segments. Then *just start* on step one.

Causes	Solutions
10. Bad habits	Replace your bad habits with good ones. Make automatic and habitual as many useful actions as you can. This frees the mind for more productive work. To acquire a new habit, launch the practice as strongly as possible. Announce it to discourage yourself from backsliding. Never let an exception occur until the habit is firmly rooted. Seize the first possible chance to act on your resolution.

Socializing

Causes	Solutions
1. Need to change pace occasionally and desire for change of scenery	Control the urge, and when indulging in it be thoughtful of others. Don't interrupt them. Breaks should be taken where no one is working, such as coffee shop.
2. Gregarious instinct/enjoy socializing	Recognize and channel to appropriate times such as coffee breaks. Stick to priorities.
3. Curiosity	Recognize and control.
4. Desire to stay informed	Plan to obtain necessary information on systematic basis.
5. Fear of offending	Be candid. Offer apologies. Suggest meeting at coffee or lunch.
6. Inability to terminate conversation	Develop techniques.
7. Inability to say no	Develop this ability. Be candid and diplomatic. Be apologetic as appropriate.
8. Thinking it is important for your business	Distinguish between keeping lines of communication open and needless socializing. Others are busy, too. Take into account that they may believe they are doing it for you. At the end of each phone call, note the effect on your business in your paper or electronic organizer, under that contact's name.
9. Boss, persistent friends	Develop subtle techniques. Remind boss of something you have to do for him. Let ap-

Causes	*Solutions*
	pearance be an indication to boss that he or she is interrupting you. Put your friends to work. Be candid. Refer to your priorities.
10. Poor physical location, heavy traffic pattern; exposed, without door or personal office	Change, if possible. Find hideaway. Do time log to show boss how location wastes time.

Staff, Inadequate

Causes	*Solutions*
1. Unaware of importance	Recognize that without competent, trained staff, effective delegation is impossible. Assign staff training an appropriate priority.
2. Remaining uninvolved or not supporting training	Recognize that both these shortcomings signal a low priority to others. A manager's involvement in training should extend two levels down for better selection of team replacements.
3. Poor selection procedures	Find out what others do. Research articles on hiring and screening procedures.
4. Lack of adequate needs assessment	The objectives and ultimately the success of a training program will depend upon the clarity with which the needs of the trainees and the organization have been assessed.
5. Lack followup	Failure to followup on training programs prevents determining the benefits achieved. Not only should measurable goals be set, but changed behavior and attitudes should be assessed at intervals following training programs.
6. Limited finances	Conduct cost-benefit analysis by logging time of those who would use additional staff. Demonstrate what additional staff would do at what cost and what those helped would accomplish in time freed up. Hire interns or form temporary partnerships on a project-by-project basis.

Causes	*Solutions*
7. Poor time use by present staff	Implement time management program targeted to save two hours per day per person. Follow up and reinforce program to gain maximum benefit. Reallocate saved time.
8. Priority projects not handled	Review case with boss and petition for increased staff. If rejected, reprioritize projects to show what can and cannot be done with limited staff.
9. Fear that only you can do the work	Recognize that if you try to do all the projects yourself, none of them may get completed.

Telephone Interruptions

Causes	*Solutions*
1. No plan for handling	Develop plan to screen, delegate, consolidate.
2. No plans for unavailability	Quiet hour; screening; set hours for taking calls.
3. Lack of delegation	Delegate more. Refer calls to delegatees. Plan calls. List points to be discussed.
4. Inability to terminate conversation	Learn, practice techniques: Preset time limit ("Yes, I can talk for a few minutes"). Foreshadow ending ("Ann, before we hang up. . . ."). Be candid ("Sorry, Joe, got to go now").
5. Ineffective screening	Analyze problem. Develop plan. Discuss with associates to avoid surprise and offense. Discuss with support staff to ensure understanding and confidence. Implement. You support your support staff!
6. No support staff	If you need your own full- or part-time staff person, do feasibility study to demonstrate need. If you have an assistant, try to use instead of new staff. If not workable, develop techniques to have messages taken at certain times. Use a hideaway. Cut-off switch. Use answering machine.

Causes	Solutions
7. "Answer your own" policy	Recognize waste of time and talent. Revise or eliminate policy.
8. Poor telephone system	Study and update. Analyze whether you need features such as automatic redial, automatic voice messaging, and caller ID.
9. No one else available to answer phones	Use answering machine. Hire high school business student or college intern who can also carry out other tasks in a mutually beneficial relationship. Ask yourself who answers when you are away.
10. Socializing to avoid dull tasks	Set daily goals for motivation. Be creative in finding a challenge.

Travel

Causes	Solutions
1. Purpose unclear	Clarify purpose, objectives.
2. Not exploring alternatives	Explore alternatives to travel, such as bringing other person to you, telephone, conference call, video conferencing, e-mail, letter, postponing, or combining with later trip. Delegate trip (send representative).
3. Forgetting to take important items with you	Develop "Take Along" list for trips. List standard items you always need; add specific items needed for particular trips as they occur to you. Put list in view where you will see it and can easily add items. Develop a to-do list for your travel time and a reward you do *not* give yourself if you then spend the travel time daydreaming.
4. Poor use of time en route	Keep folder for Reading, Writing, or Discussion (public transportation). Keep lists for Thinking, Planning, Dictation, or Tapes for Listening (driving).
5. Poor scheduling	Schedule for optimum results. Consider (a) timing (potential of visit; availability and readiness); (b) barriers (weather, traffic, construction, speed limits); (c) routing (geographic distribution, location regarding other prospects).

Causes	*Solutions*
6. Stacked desk upon return	Devise plan with support staff to handle work in your absence. Determine amount of responsibility and authority that can be delegated. Assistant could send/phone list or copies of correspondence; instructions for response could be phoned in or put on dictation machine. Laptop computer could transmit information to office periodically.
7. Changing or re-scheduling trip	Confirm all appointments before making travel arrangements. Use travel agent.

Appendix B

Electronic Time Management

Time has not speeded up, but *change* has. Time managers must now add to their challenges the mastery of new information, new machines, and new technology at breathtaking speed. This means there is more to absorb, more to learn, and more to manage—but in the same amount of time.

Since we cannot get more time, we must learn to *choose.* This is fundamental. People think they cannot choose, but if they do not, they will drown. Not only must they develop a method for choosing, they must develop a system for deciding what *they will do themselves* and what they will *delegate.* Then they must *plan and organize.* Keeping track of all these functions, keeping track of all the people they deal with, and applying the principles in this book can be done (1) in their heads, (2) on paper, (3) electronically, or (4) by using some combination of the three.

In the days when many people's lives were centered in smaller communities or urban neighborhoods, these functions could be managed very effectively in their heads, with a little help from paper. Today many of us meet new people every day from all over the country and all over the world, until our personal and professional relationships number in the thousands. This fact places most of us, every day, in the same situation as Robert Frost, who had "miles to go and promises to keep" before he could sleep.

Today we think of keeping track as "contact management" or "relationship management." Numerous paper and electronic systems have been devised to help us carry out these activities effectively.

While your first reaction may be that such systems are cold, impersonal, and reduce human relationships to information on a computer screen, the alternative can be even worse. Leaving a raft of broken promises, missed appointments, and lost telephone notes in our wake is enough to send most of us screaming to the nearest paper or electronic organizer. Originally, the telephone answering machine and the computer were viewed with suspicion, as fostering impersonal, cold interactions. Now many people value answering machines as a way to conduct business efficiently when they *want to conduct business,* and a way to free up telephone time for those occasions when they *want to interact personally.*

The total effect of computers and the Internet on human relationships is a complex subject widely discussed in many disciplines and extends beyond the time management scope of this book. But electronic time management is now a fact of life. It includes hardware, software, and a range of devices that interface with each other. It comes complete with major advantages and major potential time wasters. Before rushing out to buy the nearest electronic or paper system, invest some time to consider the following questions:

- What are the advantages and disadvantages of electronic time management and paper time management? How can each kind of system help you?
- What standards of selection should you use in purchasing a system? What landmines should you watch for?
- How big is the learning curve required to get *you* up and running quickly on the system?
- How much maintenance is required?
- How difficult and how expensive is it to update the system?
- How easily can your system interface with the other systems in your life? How easily can your system interface with the systems of other people and other organizations?
- How flexible is your system as you adapt to changes in your life?
- Do you really have to throw out the whole system and start over with a new one every few years or every six

months? Or can you update the one you have without losing either your competitive edge or your composure?

- What kind of technical support is available? How much does it cost? How long does it last? How accessible is it? In some instances automatic redial systems are a necessity in order to access busy technical support lines—or even to get on line to access the "free" technical help which can answer your questions or provide free download material. Some electronic organizer systems provide automatic updates. If you subscribe to their system, they will automatically download each updated version of the software into your older version, provided you have purchased the original software.

In electronic time management, as in other areas of life, each of us has to make an assessment about how knowledgeable we need to become—and how much of the mastery of the subject we can delegate to others. This is a crucial time management issue. To what degree do you want to spend hours poring over computer manuals and installing your own internal modems? To what degree do you want to delegate these tasks to others?

The more we become experts in any area, the greater our advantage in quickly assessing solutions when trouble arises. The less we are subject to the schedules, personalities, or miscalculations of the "experts" we are relying on. The less we spend our time on hold or redialing to access busy tech support help lines. The degree to which we become experts in any area increases our control.

It also makes us slaves to information. Poring over manuals, reading every PC, Mac and Internet magazine, and mastering every new piece of software can all be tremendous time wasters. In this interdependent society, there is no way you are going to be an expert in everything. As with car care, health care, and risk management, *time* management requires an *ongoing assessment* of (1) how much research you need in order to deal with and manage the "experts" you rely on, (2) how much you can master, so you can handle certain problems quickly without calling in an expert, and (3) how much you need to keep track of the sources where you can access the information you need, without either carrying it in your head or relying on an expert. Finding the right combination of paper and electronic organizers can help you with these tasks.

In writing this portion of the revised *Time Trap,* we interviewed a number of providers of electronic time management systems. They gave the following advice:

1. Always back up your system. This is the number-one principle of electronic time management. Add it to the number-one principle of all *time* management: "Identify your real number-one priority and get it done first." Add it to the wise observation made by Rosemary Kane Carlough, manager at AMA Periodicals: "It's not a question of *whether* you will be laid off or will change jobs. It's a question of *when.*" In the case of electronic time management, it's not a question of whether a computer or a database may crash. It's a question of when.

Based on how much information you are adding and processing, determine how often you need to back up: monthly, biweekly, weekly, twice weekly, or daily. Many people back up daily. Remember, you don't have to be sitting there staring at the screen while the back-up is proceeding. Use a back-up application or simply copy the files to separate disks, label and date them, and—this is crucial—store them in a way that you and someone else you designate can easily find them.

2. How secure is the system? Before you purchase, ask the vendor to explain the level of security of the electronic time management system. How likely is it to crash? How susceptible is it to invasion—by either unwanted users or by a virus? Follow up with questions asking what kind of platform the electronic organizer is built on. What is its architecture? How robust is the database? These are important questions because the greater the degree to which the system is prone to crash, the greater your risk of being faced with time delays in (1) determining what is wrong, (2) determining whether you need to send the database in for repairs, and (3) downtime while you and your database are separated from each other.

If, in your assessment, the vendor appears reluctant, vague, confused, or irritated in answering these questions, look elsewhere. It's your time—and your life. Looking elsewhere does not mean that you're ruling out this vendor as an electronic time management source. It means that you consider your time valuable enough that you wish to make an informed choice.

3. How fast is the system? Weighing the speed of your computer, your modem, and your electronic time management system against the financial investment required to achieve a certain speed is now an economic decision which ranks right up there with whether to purchase living quarters, rent them, or build them. It's simply a matter of acquiring all the information you can muster and applying the intelligence at your command.

4. Find out if you can customize the layout and the features of the system to meet your needs, whether you're an independent professional with multiple clients or the CEO of a dynamically changing organization.

5. Ask if the system is backward-compatible as well as forward-compatible. Can it talk to earlier versions of electronic time management *and* earlier versions of word processors used by other people you interact with?

6. Determine which systems and which people you need to interface with. Then ask the vendor to detail how you will interface with each of these.

7. Ask how competent, how fast, how long-lasting, and how expensive the technical support is.

8. Set up your computer to check for viruses every time you boot up. This can be well worth the time investment if you compare it to the havoc which can be wreaked in your life by corrupt data.

9. Most paper systems require little learning time. You pick up a pencil and write. To make a change, you erase. Or you insert a fresh sheet in your loose leaf organizer notebook. You take with you only those sheets you need, in the traveling version of your organizer. Ask the vendor to describe in detail how long it takes the typical user to get up and running in this specific time management program.

10. Contact management is really relationship management. People expect you to remember everything you've ever

said to them, or to be able to call up everything you've ever said or written to them. Ask the vendor to explain how this system really helps you to do this efficiently and effectively.

11. Ask what targeted marketing options exist for you within this electronic management system. How do they work and what do they cost?

Above all, insist on a specific explanation of how you can interface your electronic and paper time management systems. Can you download your electronic organizer's calendar, schedule, and contacts into any one of the standard paper organizers for those occasions when you don't want to make noise or be obtrusive taking notes during a meeting, or when you don't want to risk the loss of—or have the burden of taking with you—a laptop notebook. If you have a personal digital organizer that fits in your pocket, will your electronic organizer easily interface with it on all important information?

Remember, all electronic and paper organizers are *tools* to help you apply the classic principles of time management to your unique situation—so that you can achieve the highest personal and professional goals to which you aspire.*

*The following three people contributed generously of their time to be interviewed for the preceding section: Chris Killarney, senior vice president of sales and marketing, Maximizer Technologies; Brenda Christensen, director of public relations, Goldmine Software Corporation; and Diane Carlini, public relations manager, Symantec Corporation.

Index